Rising Strong:

MANAGING HOTELS

The Phoenix rises
from the ashes of Pandemic

RAM GUPTA

Contents

Contents

Contents

Preface

Until the beginning of 2020, the global hospitality industry was all smiles, showing record numbers of travellers, great occupancies and average rates, and healthy bottom lines. And then came the Covid-19 pandemic, and almost overnight, everything changed...

Perhaps, in the annals of history, few events have left as profound an impact on the world as the global pandemic that swept across continents, leaving in its wake a trail of loss, uncertainty, and disruption. The hospitality industry, an emblem of warmth, comfort, and shared experiences, found itself at the epicentre of this storm. Hotels stood silent, resorts lay dormant, and bustling city centres turned into ghost towns. The world, it seemed, had pressed pause on hospitality.

Yet, this is not a story of defeat. This is a tale of resilience, of the phoenix rising from the ashes. The hospitality industry, with its indomitable spirit, embraced the challenge and rewrote the narrative of not only survival but that of coming out as the conqueror of a war. It is a testament to the unwavering determination and innovative thinking, against all odds, that allowed this industry to not just weather the storm but emerge stronger and more adaptable than ever before.

But amidst the darkness, glimmers of hope emerged. The hospitality industry, renowned for its ability to cater to the ever-changing needs of its guests, swiftly pivoted to meet the demands of the times. With agility and determination, hotels transformed into safe havens, implementing rigorous health and safety protocols to protect guests and staff alike. A new definition of hospitality evolved, encompassing not just warm smiles and impeccable service but also a commitment to the well-being and peace of mind of all who crossed their thresholds.

Innovation became the rallying cry of the industry. From contactless check-ins to creative outdoor dining experiences, from virtual tours to personalised experiences delivered to guests' doorsteps, hotels and resorts embraced technology and creativity like never before. The human spirit, driven by a desire to connect and create memorable experiences, found new avenues to flourish even amidst physical distancing.

Today, the world has gradually opened up, and we embark on a new chapter. It is with renewed hope and inspiration that we reflect on the trials and tribulations faced by the hospitality industry during the pandemic years. This book honours the spirit of those who refused to yield, who embraced change, and who crafted a path towards recovery.

May these pages stand as a testament to the unwavering spirit of the hospitality industry—a spirit that teaches us that even in the face of adversity, innovation and determination can light the way forward. As we turn these pages, let us remember that hope springs eternal and that the transformative power of hospitality knows no bounds.

In the following chapters, you will explore the remarkable actions and strategies adopted by the hospitality industry and individuals who overcame the greatest challenge of our time. Their journeys will inspire, uplift, and remind us that the human spirit, fuelled by unwavering passion, can weather any storm and emerge stronger on the other side. Managing hotels in the post-pandemic era has redefined the industry!

Welcome to the hospitality industry—the industry that not only survived but thrived in the face of adversity.

Remember, we care!

"The buyer is entitled to a bargain.
The seller is entitled to a profit. So there is a fine
margin in between where the price is right.
I have found this to be true to this day whether
dealing in paper hats, winter underwear or hotels."

– Conrad Hilton

Employee Mental Well-Being: Unrealistic Expectations in Hospitality Need to Check-Out Permanently

Working in the hospitality industry is demanding in more ways than one. But physical rigours of the role aside, employees undergo immense emotional and mental strain. To ensure the mental well-being of their employees, hoteliers must begin by acknowledging that there is a deep-seated problem that needs to be addressed from the core.

The hospitality industry is home to some of the most hard-working professionals, who are trained to deliver in times of duress. At the very onset of their careers, they are taught to embrace the prevailing mantra of 'always at your service, with a smile'. And a spirit of working in a pressure-cooker atmosphere is deeply ingrained in them, irrespective of their job profiles. Every hospitality professional, at some point or other, has to respond to incidents beyond their control, manage crises, and outperform themselves to live up to workplace demands. However, what at first looks like a challenge or opportunity to outshine others soon turns into an irrepressible stressor they don't know how to deal with or overcome. The pressure they undergo becomes an undeniable part of the job, and the implications of the prolonged stress, added to unhealthy ways of handling it, become so aggravated that their mental well-being deteriorates.

Prioritising Mental Health: Long Overdue

As unfortunate as it may be, the hospitality sector has miles to go where caring for its own is concerned. Far from providing the resources to help deal with the prolonged exposure to comes-with-the-job pressure, many decision-makers are yet to acknowledge that a change is required. Players in hospitality have always needed a better track record in providing a work-life balance to their workforce. The prevalence of irregular sleeping patterns, disorderly eating habits, and unhealthy lifestyle practices have been overlooked for ages. What's even worse is that the industry attributes this imbalance to the nature of the business and continues demanding employees to spend at least 10 hours a day at work, with shifts easily going up to 16–17 hours in peak seasons. While burnout is the obvious consequence, the unsound practices have a domino effect, from which only a few can recover without help.

Many employees live through anxiety and depression that go completely unnoticed because everybody has to be on their toes, serving without complaints. The physical strain and emotional distress they go through to meet the expectations trigger dependency on intoxicants to take the edge off. If anyone falls short of delivering as expected, they face backlashes that further weaken their mental health. Sadly, the declining mental health of employees and the inability of the higher-ups to recognise and address the provoking factors are two major reasons why the industry also has a conspicuously high rate of alcohol consumption and substance abuse.

Expectations: The Root of Mental Ill-Being

Many of the mental health conditions faced by workers in the hospitality industry arise because they are subjected to a series of unrealistic, sometimes unattainable, expectations. The industry needs to put an end to factors that sprout unrealistic expectations and replace the older ways of operation with a more accommodating, empathetic one. Meeting organisational goals, serving guests, or acquiring professional targets should not be accomplished at the expense of mental health. The industry must channel its energies towards understanding what causes negative effects on the well-being of its people. And that begins with hotels cleaning house, flushing out the alarming components, and being reasonable with what they are asking of their staff.

- *Meeting the organisation's expectations must be gratifying, not taxing.*

Hotels have been functioning on a 'guest over employees' mindset for a seemingly endless time. Unfortunately, an industry that deals with providing services in person has a deep-rooted toxic culture within. There have been uncountable instances when superiors abused their power, manipulated or intimidated their junior team members, and completely disregarded their emotional and psychological well-being. By the time one realises the exploitation they have been suffering, they are on the verge of a breakdown. Only a few pick themselves up to raise a concern or complaint. Others simply give up and leave. The distress of the entry-level workforce is even more appalling. They have to put up with a toxic work environment with little to no scope for upskilling in the initial years of their career. Their remunerations are lower than in any other industry, and they must sweat blood to meet expectations.

Hoteliers must stop burdening employees with overwhelming expectations and asking them to slog through hours on end. The enormous stress they endure is enough to push them over the edge, yet they always come through as humanely and politely as possible. But they hardly get the benefit of the doubt, a margin of error, or management support when they are at the receiving end of things. A hotel's leadership needs to treat employees with kindness, even if they sometimes falter. Only then can a culture with strong values, less stress, and greater employee morale be built. Only then will employees enjoy working in such an organisation.

- ***Living up to guest expectations must bring joy, not stress.***

The hospitality industry is not unaware of guests' demanding behaviour. Now and then, a hotel encounters a guest who makes unrealistic requests, throws a tantrum, or creates a scene when those requirements are not delivered on the dot. Believe it or not, customers overstepping boundaries and intimidating staff to engage with them are much more common in the hospitality sector than in any other service industry. In several cases, hoteliers tolerate such behaviour because they do not want to lose the client or let the incident impact the impression of the property. Sadly, staff abuse is a reality that many hotels often keep under the hat. Not only do they overlook the detrimental effect such an occurrence may leave on a person's mental health, but they also tend to minimise the issue if an employee attempts to file a report.

Meeting the expectations of difficult customers is always challenging, but it can be done if a hotel's staff works smart. But expecting them to weather through abusive ones is a pure lack of governance guidelines. There are times when a staff member might have to pull out all the tricks up their sleeves so the guest experience is not affected. But the question is, at what price? One might argue that they work in shifts. Sure. But they do not get to switch off even when they are off duty. They have to be available 24x7 and run to the rescue whenever needed. More so if the hotel runs on a lower staff-to-key ratio or is short-staffed. As such, a hotel must have policies to help employees rest, recuperate, and regain their physical, emotional, and mental strength before returning to work.

- ***Fulfilling professional expectations must be satisfactory, not a matter of worry.***

Like any other working professional, people in the hospitality industry strive to be dexterous and completely present on the job. They, too, tend to ignore their well-being because they feel obligated to the responsibilities they are entrusted with, which is to ensure that guests receive the best of services and experiences. They wear themselves to a shadow, constantly wanting to make their clients happy. Many also associate their self-worth with the appreciation they receive from guests. In the process, they set in motion a vicious cycle of pleasing others and finding validation. They push themselves to work extra shifts, and on day offs, to chase gratification. What they do not comprehend is that constantly being out there all the time also takes a toll on their mental health—the mind needs to switch off to relax, absorb the calmness, and rejuvenate itself.

While one part of a person's mind will always desire to perform better, the other part will crave rest. Not allowing themselves to take time off can be extremely counterproductive in the long run, giving rise to an internal conflict that will manifest as job anxiety, discontentment, and never-ending trepidation. It is crucial for a person working in hospitality to draw the line when required because the job will always demand more. Understandably, professional growth and personal appeasement are great motivators to work hard, but one can only serve with joy if their inner self is at peace. Professionals in the hospitality industry must also prioritise their mental well-being as much as their organisation is expected to care for them.

Look Within: It's Time to Change

The hospitality industry has to become proactive in prioritising its employees' emotional and mental health. It must accept that the working conditions are, indeed, hectic and demanding. It needs to acknowledge that workplace stress impacts employees' mental well-being in far more ways than imaginable and stop pushing employees to remain amiable at the cost of their health. Everybody in the chain of command must pay close attention to the human capital it so dearly relies upon and prevent their well-being from going down the rabbit hole. And having done that, they should also put in place a well-designed self-development program that empowers employees and teaches them to manage work stress efficiently. Furthermore, a support system that creates a safe space for employees to vent and share their emotions can also help them unwind.

For an industry that takes pride in catering to the joy and happiness of people and providing calm and relaxing spaces for guests, hospitality needs to look inward, transform, and get better at showing love toward its own people.

Digital Marketing: Four Questions Hotels Should Ask Themselves

Over the years, digital marketing has become a powerful tool that a brand can leverage to boost visibility and drive sales. And to ensure that your marketing strategy yields the best results, it's important to have a strong purpose and vision for it, which can happen by asking the right questions.

Digital marketing holds inimitable benefits for hotels, just like it does for any business worldwide. From creating brand awareness to managing reputation, the right strategies can help hoteliers reach, connect, and create and maintain a relationship with a global audience. They can directly engage and interact with their audience by streamlining their marketing efforts and maintaining an always-on approach without spending a fortune. A hotel's digital presence can draw the attention of potential consumers towards the brand and aid in its sustainability and growth.

Chances are that you are already maintaining a presence in the digital space and adhering to all or some of the best practices to boost your visibility on digital media.

- Your website is well-developed and engaging.

- You have listed your hotel on search engines and digital publications.

- You are creating content to highlight the finest features of your hotel.

- You are regularly posting on social media platforms.

- You are regularly launching email campaigns.

- You are running digital ads, too.

- You might have even tried your hand at influencer marketing.

However, the question is whether you are utilising the available digital tools to their full potential. Read on to learn how you can leverage digital marketing to attain your hotel's business goals rather than simply being present online.

Are You Talking to Your Target Audience?

Consider this: You have a fantastic idea that will shatter the glass ceilings of hotel digital marketing. You've invested your time, energy, and resources to develop and launch a foolproof campaign. You know what and where you are marketing it. You have a robust strategy in place. But you did not identify or define your target audience. The result? You end up pushing your hotel and services to people who are not interested in what you have to offer. While growing your consumer base and creating intrigue for attracting new audience sets is important to expand the business, marketing yoghurt to a lactose-intolerant audience is a waste of effort, no matter how fancy!

If yours is a young, vibrant place with facilities for brilliant nightlife, the ideal approach is to promote your property to a younger demographic. Suppose your hotel is located in an exotic, remote location, where the entire town sleeps by supper time, then your communication must target an audience who wishes to escape the hue and cry of their busy lives. Recognising your target audience will make your message relevant and more meaningful. Only then will your digital marketing efforts yield the desired results.

What Are You Selling?

The purpose of devising any marketing plan is to communicate with your audience—your past, present, and future guests—about the services your hotel extends. But you aren't the only hotel reaching out to that target group. Your competitors are talking about the world-class facilities and amenities fitted into their property. They, too, are selling comfort after a long day of travel. They are also talking about competitive price policies. To stand out from the rest, you have to advertise what makes your property unique—why is your hotel the most fascinating option?

Now, the distinct attributes of a hotel will vary from another. A city hotel can have technological solutions that others still need to implement in their hotels. Another may have a restaurant with a unique menu. A resort in a remote location can curate activities and experiences exclusive to its in-house guests. Another may highlight their contribution to the socio-economic environment of the local community. The unique experience of your hotel can range from the minutest things, such as the high key-to-staff ratio, to larger ones like sustainability efforts, from local sourcing of ingredients to solar energy, from pet-friendly accommodation to special activities for children. As a hotelier, you must evaluate your strengths and promote the sui generis or nothing-like-it experiences and stories on digital platforms.

When Does the Experience Begin?

A guest's journey with your hotel commences long before their actual journey begins. It starts when your hotel pops up in that initial research as they zero down on the destination for their next trip. Optimising your website and blog content to appear at the top of the list is great. But what happens when they click and enter your digital space? Are you bombarding them with endless keywords?

While you have to bring out your key value propositions, focusing on what your audience wants to hear rather than basing your content on what you have to say is important. With your curated content, you must create a personal connection as you cater to the needs and desires of the travellers. Make your content relatable, as if your audience is discussing their travel plans with a close friend who's also an experienced traveller. You must ensure that visiting your website, surfing through your social media handles, and reading your profile on listing platforms is a delightful experience. Your digital space is the first touch point for your future guests. As such, it must be a virtual front for all the seamless experiences you have in store.

Must the Journey End?

Hoteliers asking guests for a rating or review on listing sites is now standard practice. A good testimonial by people who have experienced your hotel is a wonderful way to flaunt the quality of your services. But your digital journey with your customers continues. This is a stage in the customer journey when you can connect with them by opening a line of direct communications.

A well-thought-out email marketing strategy can help you maintain a long-lasting relationship with your past customers and inspire them to recommend your hotel to their friends and family. You can stay in touch, greet them on special occasions, send offers and updates, share news about your region, engage them with engaging and interactive content, and so on.

When travellers choose your property for their holidays, you become an integral part of their story. Your efforts to form or maintain a relationship with them must not end with them checking out of your hotel. Getting your digital marketing strategies can empower you to do more. It can help you persuade guests to return to your hotel over and over again!

"The Customer is Never Wrong"

– César Ritz

Reducing Employee Turnover: What Hotels Can Do to Boost Retention

Worried about employee turnover that's draining your resources? Does your team have one foot out of the door already? Here are some tips that will get them to stay while fostering a work culture they'd be proud to be a part of!

In the hospitality industry, high employee turnover and understaffing are major concerns. Some establishments face an annual turnover as high as 94%, and the two main positions that are most commonly understaffed are front-of-house and back-of-house hourly positions. At this juncture, the important question that most hoteliers are asking themselves is: *How can we reduce employee turnover and retain the employees we've already got?* Here are some solutions to this problem.

First Things First: What's Causing Your Employees to Leave?

There could be any number of reasons why your employees are throwing in the towel and walking away. Understanding these reasons, along with observing the ones that are cropping up more often than others, could be an important step in reducing employee turnover.

For instance, if your data reveals that a large number of your employees are leaving because they were brought in on false expectations, you would instruct your hiring manager to be more honest in conveying the KPIs, growth prospects, and earning potential of the role at hand. Or, if you discovered that lack of training and growth opportunities were leading to dissatisfaction, you would pour resources into employee training and development to boost the retention rates.

Data is power. You cannot change something that you haven't studied or monitored. So, make the effort to understand why your employees are leaving by using surveys and exit interviews to gather qualitative data.

Foster a Culture of Transparency

Countless surveys across different organisations have revealed that employees value a transparent organisation over one that prefers to keep their cards too close to their chest. In fact, obscurity and ambiguity within the organisational structure were identified as among the top reasons why employees preferred to quit.

Transparency is crucial—not just for employee retention but to create a healthy work culture in general. When you hire someone, he isn't just entering into a work contract with you; he's signing a bond of trust with you, and when you keep information from them, it eats away at that trust.

I am not saying that you have to share everything with your employees, including that top-secret hotel acquisition you are planning next year. But constantly ask yourself, "Is there a good reason why this information has to be kept secret?" If you can't come up with anything substantial, let the information flow freely. This will help employees contribute and collaborate with you better and also foster a culture of openness.

Have a Strong Onboarding Process

No matter how many years of experience you may have under your belt, joining a new company is always tough. There are so many things one has to learn—about the organisation, its values, your role within it, the HR policies, and even the specific goals they'll be working towards. Given that there's a whole lot of information to disseminate and process, you should have a seamless process to onboard your new employees.

When mapping out your onboarding process, include a variety of information within it. In addition to details about your HR policy and company rules, also include information about a bunch of other things, like core values, incentives, appraisal, chances of professional development, and opportunities for learning and skill-building. Also walk them through any expectations you may have from them, along with training regarding employee sensitivity and sexually appropriate behaviour.

A robust onboarding process can help your employees transition into a new place with the least discomfort and settle into their new roles with ease.

Finally, Train Your Managers

There's a very popular saying I've come across many times: "Employees don't quit jobs, they quit bad managers," and in my experience in the hospitality industry, I've found that there's a lot of truth in this wise adage.

Let's not deny reality: A lot of managers fail to make their team feel respected and safe. It's extremely important for you to conduct leadership development training that will give managers the skills to communicate, motivate, and manage their teams well. Managers and leaders are meant to encourage the people working under them and ensure that they're happy and enjoy their jobs. However, not everyone may be born ready for this role, and some training could really help them move in the right direction.

Focused training can help create managers who bring about positive changes in the company, establish a great work culture, boost job satisfaction, and engage employees meaningfully. Studies show that training specifically related to leadership development and human resource management could reduce turnover rates by 25–35%.

Employee turnover can significantly drain a company's resources, and with all the chaos that already plays out inside a hotel, this is one less worry that you could do without, right? So take decisive steps to study and reduce employee turnover and create a company that everyone would like to stick around in.

Hotel Property Management Systems: Undeniably Critical for Your Business

Managing a property in today's dynamic scenario takes a lot more than you can imagine. Hotel property management systems (PMS) play a vital role in supporting the management in keeping your business up and running. It offers hoteliers the power to improve operating efficiency and deliver exceptional guest experiences.

The modern hospitality landscape is quite different from what it used to be. Customers expect hotels to be efficient and pick up the pace with their daily operations and processes to meet their demands. A hotel Property Management System (PMS) can be of great help in such a scenario.

Modern PMSs are equipped with cutting-edge technology that helps hotels automate and streamline daily operations and improve efficiency for maximising customer satisfaction and revenue. From booking to final billing, PMS enables both small and multi-city hotels to comfortably manage their front desk operations, internal workflow, and customer data

Here's how PMS assists hoteliers in running their business successfully:

Structured solutions: By automating basic functions, such as information sharing and sending alerts, PMS creates opportunities for the staff to serve their guests better. By implementing PMS, you can reduce manual work to a great extent. In some cases, it reduces, or even eliminates, the time spent on lengthy tasks and operations, allowing hoteliers to focus on the guests and their needs.

Transparent communication: Clear communication between different teams of a hotel is essential. It helps them work in sync and serve guests optimally. PMS provides scope for direct communication among all the teams, ensuring the effective and efficient operation of the hotel. Most importantly, it saves time and offers guests an improved and more personalised experience.

Sophisticated revenue tactics: By keeping track of Key Performance Indicators (KPIs), PMS allows hoteliers to implement effective data-driven revenue management strategies. Tracking indicators, such as Average Daily Rate (ADR), Revenue Per Available Room (RevPAR), and Gross Operating Profit Per Available Room (GOPPAR), help hoteliers understand revenue flow and performance while facilitating better business decisions.

While these are a few points on how PMS helps in the efficient functioning of a hotel, here's how it supports the hotel staff in daily operations.

Front desk staff: Using PMS, a hotel's front desk staff can streamline the reservation process. Right from accepting bookings (coming via walk-ins, travel agents, or over-the-air [OTAs]) and assigning rooms to sending out confirmation emails to guests, everything is just a few clicks away. The same goes for booking cancellations/ modifications and room upgrades.

Help staff in guest registration: Apart from recording guest details, such as full name, type free individual traveller (FIT) or corporate, gender, nationality, and contact details, PMS also records guests' preferences on aspects like food, payment modes, and rooms booked during their previous stay. Such details can help you understand and serve them better in the future.

Help staff in night audit through MIS: For night audits, PMS automatically posts room tariffs and taxes on the guests' folios by confirming and reconciling the final balance of the entire day's transactions. Similarly, you can track, evaluate, and determine the performance of your business from monthly, quarterly, and annual Management Information System (MIS) reports. PMS also provides accurate and comprehensive statistical data for forecasting and budgeting so that businesses can offer services at competitive prices.

Housekeeping staff: The standard of housekeeping plays a vital role in ensuring guest satisfaction. The front desk staff can mark rooms as 'vacant' post-checkout on PMS and send an alert to the housekeeping department. Similarly, the housekeeping staff can mark the room as 'available to occupy' after cleaning. This results in faster check-in and check-out for guests along with a seamless flow of information between the departments.

Point-of-sales staff: Guests don't just stay in their rooms; they often use the bar, restaurant, gym, spa, and other facilities as well. There are different Points of Sale (POS) that can share information about the customers and deliver a tailor-made experience. In such a scenario, POS staff can update a guest's POS charges/non-room charges directly to their tabs. This way, the guest can pay the total bill in one go while checking out. PMS and POS integration help save time and avoid billing errors at the same time.

Increasingly disruptive innovations and advanced technologies have changed the way hoteliers run their business. From artificial intelligence to robots and virtual reality, advancements in PMS software will further help hotels multiply their revenue and serve their guests better.

"If you cannot make it greater, at least preserve it. Do not let things slide. Go on doing my work and increasing it, but if you cannot, do not lose what we have already done."

– Jamsetji Tata (Taj Hotels)

RevPAG: The New-Age Performance Metric that's Coming into its Own

A hotel's RevPAR effectively measures its revenue performance but does not provide an elaborate picture of the revenue sources and the overall performance of a hotel's varied departments. Nor does it give any insights into the additional activities and experiences a hotel offers. RevPAG, on the other hand, is more detailed as a metric as it shifts the focus from earnings from available rooms to spending by available guests.

Revenue per available room (RevPAR) has been a longstanding performance measurement metric the hotel industry relies upon. It has been an effective tool for analysing where a hotel stands and what could be the next course of action to improve the numbers. So far, RevPAR has helped hotels optimise their resources through fluctuating demands and seasonalities. Hotels have also learnt to maximise revenues through well-developed room allocation strategies—distributing the rooms based on the category of guests or bookings. Studying their RevPAR, hoteliers have been able to stay ahead of their competitors. However, this standardised practice of gauging performance barely takes into account anything other than the number of rooms a hotel has to offer. The industry needs to transition to a more comprehensive yardstick for evaluation and forecasting. Moving to Revenue Per Available Guests (RevPAG) can be the next step for hotels.

What exactly is RevPAG?

RevPAG stresses the proceeds from guest experiences rather than limiting the calculations to occupied rooms. An evolved form of the much-valued RevPAR used by the hospitality industry, RevPAG considers the entire lifecycle of your hotel's guests—from the moment they muse about their travels until they return home. In this period, you are presented with several opportunities to capitalise on a traveller's willingness to spend. RevPAG capitalises on that readiness and focuses on how and where a guest spends before, during, and after their stay.

While your hotel's inventory is and will continue to be a major contributor to your RevPAG, the ancillary services and experiences are instrumental in determining your hotel's overall performance. RevPAG emphasises that you journey with your guests through the pre-purchase, consumption, and post-purchase stages. In other words, every way your hotel can elevate the quality of experiences, add value to a guest's travel experience, and earn from them must be encompassed in your performance metric—your RevPAG.

Why RevPAG and not RevPAR?

Hospitality has come a long way from just providing clean rooms and parking spaces to visitors. Travellers, too, have evolved over the years. The new legion of travellers is more likely to choose experiential hotels for their vacations—room tariffs are only the first point of deliberation in their selection process. Today, people want hoteliers to participate equally in making their holidays memorable. They would not shy away from spending more if your hotel offered add-ons to make their stay more exciting and special. Many travellers would not even mind if you provided an all-inclusive package for them as long as their experience is worthwhile.

Moreover, you cannot deny that the actual time guests spend in their rooms is much less than what they spend outside. Irrespective of whether they are leisure or business travellers, it is highly likely that they will step out of their quarters for one reason or another—be it an afternoon in your hotel's coffee shop, a relaxing day by the pool, or an excursion to a nearby attraction. They will always look for other options to enjoy during their stay. As such, your hotel's performance measurement must include factors other than the rooms they occupy. Doing so will also enable you to bring the different departments of your hotel under one umbrella while examining revenue performance.

For example, suppose your limited-period coffee shop has been doing well recently. In that case, you can consider extending its hours of operation or adding more items to its menu. If your concierge desk has been receiving more requests, you can make provisions for expanding your fleet. And when you sit down to evaluate your hotel's performance, all the income centres come together to give you an exhaustive RevPAG.

How Can You Achieve Better RevPAG?

Your hotel's inventory is absolute, and guests per room are variable. So are the guests' expectations and the experiences they seek. You must always be mindful of this while attempting to improve your hotel's RevPAG. There's no doubt that your hotel's add-ons must cater to the convenience and interests of your guests. Your rooms are the baseline upon which your hotel's revenues are generated. But there is always scope to upsell a higher category once the guests have checked in. And you must aim to supplement the income generated by cross-selling the facilities and experiences you have developed in and around your property. Your guest relationship team must apprise guests of the various add-ons you are equipped to provide.

While you have to look at diversifying the income centres of your hotel to accomplish higher RevPAG, your offers must also appeal to the novelty of your guests. Think of different ways to engage your guests—in-house and in your area of operations. Identify unique activities and create special packages around them. Something as simple as an alfresco dinner on your hotel's rooftop can be your hotel's sui generis. If you are located in smaller towns and remote locations, you have greater elbow room to curate all-inclusive packages your guests won't be able to deny. Take boutique wildlife lodges, for example. A majority of them sell on a per-person, per-night basis. Their tariffs include meals, safaris, day guides, and local experiences. Some also offer transport services to and from the nearest airports and railway stations. Although the earnings of such properties may be seasonal, they leave no stone unturned to maximise their RevPAG. And people still buy them because the guest experiences they offer are one-of-a-kind.

RevPAG works as a performance metric and helps hotels shift their attention from rooms to guests. It brings personalised services and experiences to the table and enables hotels to meet guest expectations. It also gives a complete analysis of the various guest assistance departments, which can help hotels make informed decisions to minimise cost centres and increase the capacities of well-performing, income-generating ones. The concept of RevPAG is not brand-new in hospitality—it has been around for a couple of years. But now, it is time for hoteliers to unleash its full potential.

Hotels Carve Out Their Slice of the Big Fat Indian Wedding Industry

The hospitality sector in India has always benefited from the revenue generated by the wedding industry. There may be fewer guests at weddings now, but the grandness of celebrations remains intact. Destination weddings, too, are on the rise. Irrespective of the size or location of a wedding, Indian couples and families still do not mind spending a fortune for a marriage ceremony. The hospitality industry can leverage a great deal from the ever-growing wedding industry.

If there's a once-in-a-lifetime celebration that Indians will happily go all-out for, it's weddings. The good news is that the hospitality sector has always grabbed a fair share of the wedding industry's earnings. From grand destination weddings to smaller banquet hall reservations, and luxury reception parties to booking catering services, weddings rope in several services from the hospitality segment. And in a country with a thriving young population, the trend of hotels hosting weddings is here to stay.

Wedding Bells Bring Revenue Flow

The business of weddings is a conglomeration of many small and big segments coming together to form one grand industry. It is observed that the must-have hospitality services—catering and venue arrangements—count for a significant share of the total expenditure in a wedding. Top that with decor and entertainment, and the numbers jump even higher. Indians have a greater willingness to spend on weddings as compared to any other celebrations. With lakhs of knots tied yearly, that brings a significant amount to the basket. This billion-dollar industry, despite witnessing a slowdown, provided a forlorn hope to hotel businesses during the shaky days of the pandemic.

Fast forward to the concluding months of 2022. The number of marriages solemnised in merely two months aided a massive turnover for the wedding industry. And it resulted in becoming a remarkable source of income for hoteliers. For some hotels, the revenue generated from wedding bookings was much higher than that of regular bookings. Considering that the wedding market is set to boom even further, India's hospitality industry will continue to benefit from it.

Fewer Guests, Grander Celebrations

The sentiment of sharing the big day with loved ones is so strong that Indians

splurge a major portion of their lifetime earnings on their 'big day'. Neither

lockdowns nor travel restrictions could restrain Indians from celebrating the most important day of their lives. Most couples went ahead with their wedding plans even during the pandemic, despite the mandates of an extremely downsized guestlist.

However, this also led to a shift in the wedding ecosystem. The hosts are not shying away from spending big bucks to make the ceremonies extravagant and memorable. People are now inclined towards intimate events with fewer guests but a better guest experience. Wedding planners and clients focus on premium experiences—comfortable stays, curated functions, personalised services, grander decor, elaborate menus, unique entertainment, hygiene and safety, and everything that prioritises quality over quantity. While weddings may be smaller, the glamour and grandeur of the celebrations are larger. The only difference is that now people are looking at celebrating their special day in a more close-knit environment in the most luxurious way they can.

Destination Weddings Are on the Rise

The mountains, heritage hotels, and popular beaches are the three top choices for destination weddings. Still, a younger generation of soon-to-be-weds is also exploring alternate options that offer a more private set-up for their big day. And the older generations are supporting them. A majority of Indian families are willing to take the wedding to a destination away from home. Hotels have observed that the demand for destination weddings is indeed increasing with venue request for proposal (RFP) being at the top of the list of enquiries for hotels.

Contrary to popular opinion, India is the most preferred destination for weddings globally. But for a long time, destination weddings were synonymous with weddings abroad—something only the elite with high spending capacity could experience. However, with intimate weddings with slimmer guest lists combined with hoteliers in different destinations offering wedding packages, Indians are rediscovering the country's resources in a new light.

Your Hotel: A Wedding Venue

When it comes to weddings, every hotel has a space or service they bring to the table. However, in an attempt to leverage the highly lucrative wedding market, hoteliers must not fall short of getting their services right. After all, different hotels have different value propositions. As a hotelier, you must focus on designing wedding packages that align with your operation's category and location.

Understanding your strengths and shortcomings is important before taking on wedding bookings. If you are experienced in managing events, consider providing tailor-made services or even going full service if you have the resources. If you are a beginner, you can start by standardising your base package and offering additional options to pick and choose from. If the wedding group has not chartered your hotel, ensure that the venues you set up for them are exclusive so that other guest activities do not hinder the celebrations in your hotel. This will also help you provide privacy to the non-wedding guests staying with you during the period.

A hotelier must recognise that weddings are memorable get-togethers for the guests, an opportunity for them to catch up with far-flung friends and family members. Your hotel experience can be an outstanding addition to that. In addition to providing the best of in-property services, you can also present them with the chance to make memories of their own by providing them with 'mini-holiday' experiences. You can offer special rates for ancillary services they can avail during their stay, such as exclusive alfresco dining, local experiences, excursions to lesser-known attractions in your region, and so on. Upselling experiential activities can be an additional source of revenue for your hotel.

A Word of Caution

In the recent past, wedding and peak travel seasons in India often overlap, raising the demand for hotel rooms and venues. There are times when hoteliers have to let go of other bookings because they have a wedding reservation lined up. But things are changing. I've seen that couples today do not limit themselves to the peak wedding season to take their vows.

To reap the benefits of the trend, business/city hotels, too, are considering hosting weddings as an all-season offering. While it holds the potential to bring in business during the shoulder seasons, hotels committing to a large inventory of rooms for a wedding party during peak season can be counterproductive. As a hotelier, you must keep a window of three to four days before and after a wedding booking—first, to make the necessary arrangements for the event; second, to tidy up afterwards to prepare your hotel for the next set of guests. That easily counts for a week's worth of hidden costs and revenue losses. Not to mention that it takes time to fill the available rooms in case the wedding groups cancel their bookings. Your booking and cancellation policies for weddings must have provisions to protect you from the consequences.

Weddings are not just a celebration of personal moments for Indians. They are a social event, a festivity. It is one segment of businesses in India that appears to be immune to any socio-economic adversities. The culture of celebrating the happily-ever-after union is evolving, and hotels across the board are jumping on the bandwagon. The hospitality industry is not only receiving a slice of the earnings of the wedding industry, but the share is also growing in size. And by being a wedding venue, hotels can become an important part of couples' lives. Hoteliers are setting the right tone for the beginning of the new phase they will embark on!

"I adapt like a chameleon to the particular society where I
am operating at the moment"

– Robert Kuok (Shangri-La)

Your hotel experience is enhanced when the staff carefully tends to your likes and dislikes. They take your preferences into account while providing their services. But as they focus on making your hotel stay top-notch, you too must be considerate about their efforts and be mindful that your behaviour does not hinder them from doing their job well.

As part of the machinery that keeps the hotel functioning like a well-oiled machine, the staff often goes beyond the call of duty to provide excellent service and meet guests' needs. Moreover, while a lot has been said about hotels doing everything to live up to guest expectations, very little is said about what the hotel staff expects from guests. Hoping for the best service from a hotel experience is not unusual. Still, many fail to understand that expectations are not a one-way street; hoteliers, too, wish for their guests to be courteous and honour the house rules during their stay at a property.

Although these may seem like small things, the impact of hotel etiquette is greatly positive. Being mindful of how you behave in a hotel helps hotel staff maintain service standards and inspires them to assist in times of need enthusiastically. Further, that culminates in making the overall experience pleasant for every guest. So, next time you are staying in a hotel, consider doing (or not doing) these things:

While in Your Room

If you arrive at a hotel's doorstep with the impression that whatever happens behind the closed doors of your room will go unnoticed, you might want to think again. Hoteliers often encounter misdemeanours and thoughtless behaviour, and many of them have the means to resolve unpleasant situations. For instance, you might think that you can get away with cheating the minibar, but hotels have learnt from bitter experiences, and they have a solution ready. They have the means to identify what has been consumed and will charge it to the guest during checkout.

If you are a smoker, the best practice is to ask for a smoking room instead of insisting on lighting a cigarette in a non-smoking room. Also, covering up the smoke alarms or cooking in a room without a proper kitchen set-up or an exhaust system are equally bad ideas, which can pose a risk to the smooth operations of a hotel by triggering the hotel's fire alarm system unnecessarily.

During my stay in hotels, I have encountered situations where my temporary neighbours have partied through the night, blasted music, slammed doors, invited unsolicited guests without informing the management, and sneaked in pets in non-pet-friendly hotels. The list goes on. You might believe that incidents like this do not happen frequently, but they are shockingly common. Moreover, these create a noisy environment and make for an unpleasant experience for other guests.

In matters of housekeeping, you might think that some of the worst nightmares for the staff are trash lying in beds, towels stained with make-up, and filthy bathroom sinks. However, things are actually worse. There have been incidents of human faeces being pushed under the rug or broken vases hidden under the mattress. Doing this can put the health and safety of the hotel staff and future guests at risk. A straightforward course of action is usually best: If you have broken a glass or damaged an electronic item, inform the staff, and they will take care of it.

While in Common Areas

Common areas in hotels are for every guest to enjoy, irrespective of the room category you or they have booked. Way back in 2015 and 2016, Expedia's Hotel Etiquette Study ranked inattentive parents as the most dislikeable category of guests in hotels. This still stands true. Having kids run around unsupervised is a nerve-wracking experience for guests and staff alike. Up there on the scale of annoyance are noisemakers who assume that quiet zones, such as hallways, lifts, lobbies, and lounges, are their personal spaces, which they can use to talk loudly and create dramatic scenes. Taking such high-volume conversations outside or into your rooms is always wiser.

When at the swimming pool, if you want to take a dip in the pool, respect the dress code and hygiene needs at the pool. Do not reserve pool loungers if you don't intend to use them anytime soon. In addition, let what happened by the pool stay by the pool. Use the shower before heading to your room instead of leaving a trail of water behind you. The same goes for when you avail spa services.

Watching your smoking habits is not limited to the four walls of your room. If you feel like smoking in one of the public areas, ensure it is not marked as a non-smoking zone. Dispose of your cigarette stubs responsibly, and never throw them in the garden, hallway, or poolside.

Being indifferent to the expected etiquette in common spaces like spas and pools directly affects the quality of the hotel experience for everyone checked into the hotel. After all, no one likes their time of peace and quiet disrupted, especially when they've come away to enjoy a pleasant vacation or business trip.

In the Case of Food and Beverages

Providing quality food and beverage facilities is integral to a good hotel experience. Staff at the hotel's restaurants and coffee shops do their best to offer diners quality experiences in these spaces. But your wayward behaviour can hinder the waitstaff from delivering the services you expect. Restless demand for their attention, snapping fingers at the staff, or sitting at a dirty table to 'hurry' things up do not fast-track the services. Instead, they put off the people who are sincerely dedicated to serving you and draw frowns from the other guests in the vicinity.

Most hotel tariffs include complimentary breakfast served in a coffee shop or banquet hall. While a breakfast-inclusive room rate allows you to eat to your heart's content, that does not mean you should be demanding takeaway boxes because you do not feel like eating breakfast! Going overboard on complimentary breakfast, crowding the buffet counters, or cutting queues to be served first only shows you in a poor light. And don't get started with your meal right next to the buffet—chances are the hotel will have seating arrangements for you to dine and indulge in discussions with your friends and family. You do not need to stand there to eat or talk, you know!

While we are on the topic of food and beverages (F&B), are you someone who places last-minute orders from your room? You might want to reconsider that habit. The hotel's F&B team will serve you, no doubt, but if you ask for room service only minutes before the kitchen closes and raise complaints when service expectations are not met, it is not entirely the hotel's fault. While the staff strives to be readily available to serve their guests, expecting them to move mountains for you is unrealistic, and frankly, ill-considered.

A larger issue with most hotel guests is disrespecting the hotel's policies and reacting in appalling ways when their behaviour is called out. Claiming more than what one has paid for, declaring 'elite' status for offers, and bickering to get discounts or upgrades are quotidian. Sometimes, hotel staff have been asked to babysit or dog sit and even blamed for unexpected weather conditions. These are outside the due services they are supposed to provide. While the hotel staff tries to treat you like an expert in cuisine, at times, it crosses the line when the chefs are called to the table to be told how to cook.

Demanding last-minute early check-ins or late check-outs and vandalising or packing up hotel property is surprisingly common, too. It is important to understand that booking a hotel room differs from buying one. A hotel lends its space, amenities, and services only for a certain period of time. But sometimes, even the most modern travellers go about with the mindset of 'paying means owning', especially when they are in their rooms. We have all been guilty of one or many of these at some point during our travels. What I am trying to say is—maybe take a step back and reconsider your behaviour. Be a better guest next time!

The Era of Smart Hotels Is Here!

Every hotelier is in a race to provide the most comfortable and satisfying stay to their customers. And with the arrival of a new generation of travellers, hotels have started using technology to stay ahead in this game. There are several different, interesting, and creative ways hotels implement technology in their properties.

Long queues at the reception, tiresome waiting for availability, and slow room service to your rooms are all things of the past. Today's modern hotels use some of the most advanced technology available to enhance customer experience like never before.

But is that the only advantage of upgrading to a smart hotel?

Ever since the pandemic, hotels have had to improve their services and find new attractions to retain customers. And one multifaceted way was to install technology. According to the recent Hotelier Technology Sentiment Report, 81.7% of hotel owners had implemented smart practices during the pandemic or were planning to do so in 2022. And since most of the technology in the new age is also made with sustainability in mind, it can boost a hotel's eco-friendly efforts.

But what does this new version of the hospitality industry look like? It can range from small things like a modern thermostat to big changes like a robot staff tending to your every need. In a hotel in Singapore, you can find robots performing tasks like room service and delivering amenities straight to the cabin. Suffice it to say that the hotel industry has changed a lot.

Let's look at some of the ways hotels use technology to enhance their services.

Conserve Energy

Advancements in technology have made it possible to automate certain aspects of the hotel that not only conserve energy but also help minimise operational costs significantly. In a recent study published in *Energies*, an open-access journal, it was found that autonomous management could save 13.19% in costs when compared to traditional manual management. And energy consumption is one of the biggest expenses in the hospitality industry.

There is a lot of room to make energy consumption more efficient. Smart thermostats, air conditioning, lighting—all these technologies can be used to not only minimise usage but also get detailed insight into how the system operates and how much energy is wasted. Many of these mechanisms use machine learning and sensors to analyse how much energy is being used, which helps in optimising the process.

Smart energy management systems are also a big help to the environment. Reducing the carbon footprint by decreasing the usage of energy can further boost the sustainability efforts of the hotel and enhance the brand image, too, making your company more likely to get picked by customers among the vast competition.

Reserve Spots

Parking is a time-consuming affair. Trying to find an empty spot can be a long wait and very frustrating for customers who are looking forward to spending their time relaxing instead of parking. It's also a huge strain on their wallets. According to a report by *USA Today,* the cost of wasted time and fuel per driver looking for a parking spot is $345 annually. But technology has found a way to solve this problem, too.

Using sensors and hotel apps to automate the process, hotels can take in reservations for parking spots for tenants and have spaces assigned to them on arrival so they don't have to drive around the lot to park their vehicles, thereby enjoying a more fluid experience. This will also save the cost of manually managing parking inventory.

Enhance Customer Experience

The most important thing a hotel needs to ensure is customer satisfaction. Nothing trumps customer reviews in the hospitality business. If your customer is unhappy with your services, it can be hard to invite new customers, let alone retain the existing ones.

Smart thermostats, occupancy reports, and efficient room service are just some of the ways technology can help to improve a customer's stay. For example, technology can help speed up the check-in and check-out processes considerably. Replacing the time taken to check availability, data entry, and long queues at the reception desk with automation, assigning rooms at the click of a button, can shave off a lot of time from the whole process.

The job doesn't end after the guests have reached their rooms. Installing voice assistants like Alexa and Google can not only be an appealing feature but also an extremely practical one. Apart from being very convenient, it also cuts back on time taken, reducing the time guests have to wait for service.

Digitise Operations

Today, our mobile phones have become key to our lifestyle. Providing access to various apps and features, the mobile has made everyday life a lot more convenient. And with technology advancing so much, the hospitality industry is also starting to involve mobile apps in their operations.

From digital room keys to one-stop access to everything that their hotel has to offer, mobile apps present a versatile option for hotels to enhance user experience. In a recent study by *Hospitality Technology*, it was stated that 73% of travellers use mobile devices to make reservations and interact with the hotel.

Using mobile apps can also boost green efforts. Reducing the manufacturing of physical keys and papers saves a lot of energy and lessens the hotel's carbon footprint.

The possibilities that technology has imparted to the hotel industry are virtually unlimited. There are some extraordinary things a hotel can do using recent innovations in technology. Take, for instance, virtual reality. Using it to conduct tours of your property can not only help appeal to more tech-savvy audiences but also give users a chance to see exactly what they will be getting in the package. A dialled-down version can be Google Street View, giving the customers spliced images in the form of a 360-degree environment of the hotel available to them on their phones.

But overloading your business with technology is not necessary. Even though technology can save a lot of money, having it installed properly is still a heavy expenditure. Automating every step of the process is not recommended, as if even one of the links in the chain breaks, the whole system could shut down. What hotels need to do is analyse what they can improve on a limited budget, what aspects to prioritise, and how many manual tasks to retain. These factors will help you decide what technology investment will drive significant returns on investments while improving guest satisfaction as well.

Can Predicting the Future Maximise Profit?

Profit maximisation is the goal of every business. And to do the same, a company uses a number of tools under their belts. Forecasting can be a useful tool if used correctly and efficiently and can help you grow your profits.

From hotels to travel advisors, every company aims to grow. It can be in size or in terms of revenue. Often, it's the latter, growth being a side effect of maximising the company's profit. And since the hospitality industry is a fast-growing one, the competition is steep, and a company should use any facilities available to them.

There are many tools to drive profit. You can increase the price of the product/service you are providing; you can increase sales through offers like 'Buy one Get one Free!', invest in marketing and social media, and so on. One such tool is forecasting.

Forecasting uses the data of past and present trends to predict the future of the company's operations accurately. Knowing how events might unfold allows a company to make decisions easily, significantly lowering risks. Forecasting can be useful to your business, helping minimise operative costs and unnecessary expenses. It can yield positive results if you know how to apply it accurately.

But why is forecasting important? The future is uncertain. And when you have a business to grow, this can be very scary. For example, a report by Skift states that hotel chains such as Marriott and Hilton aggressively pushed direct booking campaigns from 2017 to 2019. If a company had been able to predict this development by analysing the trends, it would have been easier to shift to direct channels. That's where forecasting comes in.

Increasing Profit

Most companies use multiple channels such as online travel agencies like Expedia and MakeMyTrip, direct streams like websites and apps, and metasearch engines like Google, etc., casting a wide net to gain as much traction as possible. But to maximise profit, they need to decide: Which channel gets priority?

Through forecasting, the hotel can choose the channels they want to improve and build upon to attain higher customer satisfaction, and ultimately, higher profits. For example, if you get more sales through metasearch engines, you can invest in SEO-based marketing like articles and blogs. If online agencies drive more traffic, exclusive offers and campaigns would be a good investment.

You can also look at it from the other side. The hotel can research different channels and their competitors' performances to see if these could be a good option for their services. If the competition is doing great on a platform, then, with some tweaks, you can also benefit from the channel.

Forecasting is not limited to historical data. Heavy research on global trends also works well in addition to classic forecasting. For example, in another report by Skift on global trends for 2023, it is stated that channels with a wider geographic range will see a rise in footfall on their sites. If you offer international trips and stays, you can invest in such channels extensively.

Methods of Forecasting

With different methods like time series analysis, regression method, the Delphi Method, etc., you can, to an extent, predict the future sales trajectory through each channel. The most used method is time series analysis. Time series analysis is a method that looks at historical data to predict the future. The only issue is that it looks only at the past data, assuming that the future is determined by historical data. This approach can struggle to produce accurate results for large data sets with irregular trends.

Budgeting and management software help a lot with forecasting. Using machine learning (MI) and artificial intelligence (AI) to predict future trends accurately gives you a lot of information to influence decisions to increase efficiency.

Let's take Amazon Web Services (AWS), for example. You only need to provide historical data and any additional data that may impact your forecasts. Once you input your data, AWS will automatically analyse it, identify what is profitable, and produce a forecasting model capable of making up to 50% more accurate predictions than looking at time series data alone.

Challenges You Might Face

Using software can help with the main problem of forecasting—its accuracy. An accurate forecast can help in many ways, like streamlining cash flow operations and increasing production efficiency. But an inaccurate prediction can lead you down the wrong path, influencing bad decisions and increasing loss instead of profit.

For online travel agencies, the company is just one of the many they facilitate. Chances are they can't give you data accurate down to the decimal points. And inaccurate data makes it impossible to forecast the future with precision.

To counteract this, you can boost sales via direct channels—like websites and apps through social media communications, exclusive discounts, and other marketing campaigns—and develop them to be your most profitable channel.

We talked about seeing the future using forecasting, but choosing the right channel for your business is important, too.

Here are some questions that might help when making a decision.

- What type of products/services do you sell?

- Who's your target audience?

- Where does your audience demographic prefer to shop?

- Do you want to cater to a local audience or scale up to a larger region?

- Does the channel fit your budget and align with the overall e-commerce strategy?

All these questions will help you decide the right platform to conduct business.

Forecasting can be a very helpful tool. But the heavy reliance on past data can be somewhat inconsistent with the results. If you can overcome the challenges and implement machine-learning-based software like AWS, you can use forecasting effectively to maximise profit and grow your business, making it one of the most beneficial tools in your arsenal.

How Mobile Keys Are Changing the Hospitality Industry

The hospitality industry has seen a change in tide after the Covid-19 pandemic with guests preferring contactless experiences. From mobile check-ins to virtual keys, we see why the industry needs to transition from human to technological.

One of the effects the hospitality industry felt from the Covid-19 pandemic was the need to optimise contactless and secure guest experiences. Thousands of hotels hoping to provide more personalised experiences to their guests have started relying on the latest technology, especially smartphones. Even though the use of contactless technologies is less prevalent than they were during the pandemic, most guests have now gotten used to the convenience of mobile room keys and mobile check-ins. The resulting reduced check-in durations and being able to bypass front desk interactions have been preferable to hotel guests.

What Are Mobile Keys?

Mobile keys are digital keys provided to guests at hotels directly to their smartphones, reducing the duration of check-ins and increasing customer satisfaction. Mobile keys are typically based on Bluetooth or Near Field Communication (NFC), and guests can use these by bringing their smartphones close to the locks.

These mobile keys give guests access to not only their rooms but also to amenities like the spa, pools, restaurants, and fitness centres. Along with virtual keys, the option of checking in through their phones allows guests to skip the front desk lines and go straight to their rooms without much hassle. Also, unlike key cards, most travellers carry their smartphones with them at all times and are less likely to forget their phones, decreasing the chances of being locked out of the room.

Major hotel franchises like the Marriott Group and Hilton Hotels have been phasing out magnetised key cards for mobile keys because of their reliability, efficiency, and for being sustainable alternatives. This simple technology has allowed the hospitality industry to provide guests with personalised contactless experiences. For example, the Marriott Bonvoy mobile app offers mobile check-in, mobile key, mobile chat and requests, and mobile dining.

Are Mobile Room Keys Preferable to Traditional Key Cards?

After over two years of travel ban due to the Covid-19 situation, travellers are excited to make the most of their journeys. This means wanting to spend less time checking in and more time just heading to their rooms and shaking off travel weariness. Using their smartphone-enabled keys gives guests a sense of security of having their room keys always with them and safe, and they can minimise hand-to-hand contact that comes with physical keys. In a survey conducted by Magnani Caruso Dutton Partners, a digital marketing agency, of 1,000 guests in 2013, 64% of the people opted to use their mobile devices as hotel room keys. This number rose to 73% during the pandemic.

Due to their magnetisation, key cards tend to be easily exploited or can get demagnetised over time, which means lower security and higher inconvenience for guests. Most people have their smartphones secured with passwords or pins, which gives them an added sense of security, even if they are misplaced.

From a business point of view, hotels spend a lot of money on the manufacture as well as upkeep of traditional keys or card keys. But with mobile room keys, there is no waste, maintenance, or need for disposal. Unlike key cards, mobile keys cannot be tampered with or misplaced, thus, eliminating the costs of replacement. A sustainable and cheaper option in the long run, a lot of hotel chains should start parcelling mobile keys as an attraction for potential guests.

Mobile keys also provide guests the option of online check-in, making the first experience in the hotel more pleasant and seamless. Also, employees don't have to spend time searching for stolen or misplaced keys, increasing their efficiency and reducing lost key costs for the property.

How Beneficial Is this Tech in the Long Run?

As guests are always in need of an efficient and secure experience, the hospitality industry should always strive to incorporate newer technologies that can make each guest's stay or time as convenient as possible. We've seen technologies change over time and revolutionise how the industry functions. In the same way, we can always count on something new coming up that we can use to make customers happy.

The digital convenience, sustainability, reduced costs, and efficiency that mobile keys can bring to any property will only add value to properties over the next decade and beyond. You must constantly look for ways to cater to the needs of every single guest, be it someone young, wanting the efficiency of technology, or someone older, wanting the personal touch. It is always beneficial to keep up with technology in this industry to ensure your customers are never left feeling like something needs to be added to their time as a guest.

"If Customers are treated right, they will come back"

– Bill Marriott Jr.

F&B Menu in Hotels Evolve and Become Major Revenue Drivers

While the pandemic created havoc in the hospitality industry, it also provided an excellent opportunity for food and beverage operations in hotels. F&B concepts have become more dynamic, customer-centric and responsive to post-pandemic needs. All this has resulted in F&B operations becoming a major revenue earner in hotel operations.

Excellent food and beverages (F&B) have always been an integral part of the experience that guests expect from a hotel. But F&B at hotels is no longer just a service but a strong indicator of the positioning and brand value of the hotel. For Indian hotels, F&B is slowly becoming a major revenue driver, contributing up to 50% to overall revenues. Offering good food and quality beverages isn't the only benchmark for a hotel's F&B anymore. Finer details come together to form a larger umbrella of the guest experience. Hoteliers have not shied away from innovating and finding newer ways to invite diners to their in-house dining spaces.

Here are a few things that have changed in hotel food and beverage in the recent past.

Small Menus, Smaller Portions

Epicureans often claim that designing a menu is nothing less than an art. However, unlike a piece of published art, a hotel's menu has to adapt and change according to the times and situations. While hotels traditionally offer long, intricate menus with an array of options, maintaining an inventory of ingredients is both cost- and time-sensitive, and implementing quality checkpoints is an extensive exercise. They also contribute to decision fatigue after flipping through numerous pages of food descriptions. The tiresome experience often results in guests either repeating items they have had before or going by the recommendations presented by their server. Smaller menus, on the other hand, when well-executed, offer a more personalised and easier dining experience.

The untapped potential of limited-offering menus emerged when challenges of the pandemic loomed upon the hospitality industry and compelled hotels to strategise ways to keep their spaces up and running. The call to offer limited dishes helped compensate for the shorter working hours, limited staff, supply shortages, and steep operating costs. At the same time, shifting to smaller portions, tasting menus, and food pairings helped hotels showcase the best they had to offer, keep the pricing attractive, and reduce wastage. Going small aided in optimising resources, streamlining processes, and curating high-value dishes while being innovative.

Going Beyond Food Hygiene and Safety

Although the concept of food safety has been around for a while, hotel restaurants often limit themselves to simply displaying allergen information on the ingredients. In recent years, a new wave of transparency has emerged, wherein the description of meals is more comprehensive than earlier. Restaurants are not only introducing more contemporary, healthier cuisines but also designing menus to provide nutritional facts and benefits of the dishes. They are innovating the existing menus to cater to the conscious lifestyle that consumers have shifted to. Plant-based meals, wellness menus, and creative non-alcoholic beverages are becoming popular inclusions for many in an attempt to maintain the health quotient in the menu offerings.

However, the change is not limited to what is being served. People are revisiting good old culinary traditions that offer both health and taste. Understanding this, restaurants are exploring the food heritage of their region of operations and adding local flavours to their offerings. Hotel restaurants address this by weaving stories of food culture into the diner's experience. Restaurants are diving deep to present the journey of the ingredients, blending modern and traditional methods of culinary presentations and elevating the dining experience by appealing to the need to become conscious consumers. From sourcing locally to being mindful about the carbon offset, and from environmental to socio-economic impacts, all are now becoming a part of elevated diners' experiences at a hotel restaurant.

Finally, the Digital Embrace

When the convenience of enjoying restaurant quality food in the comforts of their homes gained popularity, hotel F&B stood its ground by offering exclusive dine-in experiences to guests. However, the pandemic brought along the challenge of keeping operations up and running. Foraying into the food delivery sector was the need of the hour. Legacy brands and hospitality chains soon turned the adverse circumstances into opportunities. What came out of necessity has become a major hotel revenue source.

As the restrictions of social distancing relaxed, hotels implemented new contactless measures to ensure the safety and comfort of diners. While QR scanners for menus and digital payments became staple protocols, hotels also leapt ahead by integrating technology for table management, food pre-order, and customer relationship management.

Hotel F&B services are known to evolve from time to time. From all-day coffee shops to anytime room service, buffet meals to special serving hours, and from banquet halls to host large groups to curated spaces for alfresco dining, hotels have adapted their spaces to trending concepts to cater to the interests and demands of guests. Today, hotel F&B is a consolidation of more than one element of service. It adds value to the overall experience, not just with food and drinks but also with a detailed look at the operating principles of a hotel.

Are Hotels' Pandemic Service Cuts Becoming Permanent?

In the wake of the huge revenue setback owing to Covid-19, hotels have been cutting their services for guests, laying off their staff, and moving towards automation. However, as service cuts make way for automation and eventually revenue generation for hotels, announcing the cuts as permanent might be ambitious.

The Covid-19 pandemic has unarguably caused the hospitality sector's worst revenue dips in the last hundred years. Big hotel chains had to scrape their fund barrels while most of the smaller local hotels had to close shop. Human touch, one of the major plus points of hospitality, was being avoided. Thus, hotels had to cut short many of their services during the pandemic, both as a cost-saving measure and as a way to limit human contact. But while travellers and hospitality professionals are waiting for things to go back to normal, it might not be the 'normal' they expect.

Chris Nassetta, president and CEO of Hilton, has warned that hotels' service cuts during the pandemic might be permanent. In a recent investor call, Chris said:

The work we're doing right now in every one of our brands is about making them higher-margin businesses and creating more labour efficiencies, particularly in the areas of housekeeping, food and beverage, and other areas. When we get out of the crisis, those businesses will be higher margin and require less labour than they did pre-Covid.

Now, while this news might be slightly off-putting for travellers who were eager to travel post-Covid, it is worse for people working in the hospitality industry. And the hammering taken by the hospitality industry seems to have been passed on to customers and staff members.

During the peak of the pandemic in mid-2020, job losses in hotels rose to more than 80%. And even those who managed to hang by a thread still had pay cuts of around 50% waiting for them. Hotels had already started letting go of many customer services, including personal concierges and room services. This statement by the Hilton CEO has left experts wondering if these service cuts will be permanent in the post-Covid era.

What Service Cuts Are We Talking About?

The hospitality industry was one of the worst pandemic-hit sectors in the world. The entire functioning of the hospitality industry is heavily based on the human touch. But keeping in mind the Covid restrictions and the hesitation of human contact, hotels had to reduce their contact points to a minimum, thus pushing a heavily contact-based sector towards automation.

For this, hotels had to let go of many routine services, including room service, housekeeping, concierges, bars, and restaurants. In general, we've seen hotels eliminate daily housekeeping and cut in-room dining and serve it in to-go bags. We've also seen them eliminate in-room amenities, ranging from minibars to coffee machines. And this isn't even the beginning of it.

Big hotel chains like the Taj and ITC had to transform their services radically. Taj Hotels had to do away with its lavish buffets while also reducing its guest capacity by almost 50%. ITC Hotels, too, suspended new reservations at many hotels. All of this resulted from one of the biggest revenue declines in the last hundred years. The gravity of the loss can be perceived by the fact that Indian Hotels Co., the luxury hotel chain that owns the iconic

Taj brand, slumped to ₹3.8 billion loss in just six months by the end of 2020! This led the hotels to rethink their business models and make way for automation.

Are Hotels Moving Towards Automation?

Definitely. Testing newer trends in hotel management, big hotel chains have already started relying on automated products and services. From Alibaba Future Hotel group to the Marriott group, the use of automation has grown prominently all over the world. Hotels now have robotic concierges, automated room services, and cleaning assistants in their pipelines. We also have hotels that are switching to robots with inbuilt UV-ray cleaning systems and using the Internet of Things (IoT) in place of a human room service.

With automated check-ins and check-outs, hotels have reduced the contact points for guests, eventually shedding the use of human resources. The newly rolled out Marriott pilot program in the US features a contactless arrival kiosk that checks in guests in just three simple steps. The program also includes a new grab-and-go machine that serves breakfasts to guests. So, yes. Automation is here. And we don't think it's likely to go anywhere!

Will Everything Return to Normal?

That's a difficult question to answer, and it depends upon the definition of normal. Hotels have been trying out automated services for a while now, and these services have helped them reduce the requirement for manpower. Now, driven by huge revenue losses, hotels will look to make it up as soon as possible. They have already been laying off staff for a while now. And if there is an automated machine to replace the laid-off manpower, there's a chance that hotels are not going to hire them back.

However, strictly speaking, the competitive hospitality market (especially now) might not allow it. It boils down to a simple demand and supply logic. As the manpower is shed, the demand for automated services will rise. And frankly, not many hotels in India (apart from the big ones) are equipped to bring in automation, let alone capable of paying the price for it. And it is just a matter of time before someone starts hiring back the manpower, and the market shifts yet again.

Frankly speaking, talking about the services cut being permanent was a bit too ambitious on the Hilton CEO's part, provided this is a B2C service sector that we're talking about. Any decision that the hotels take is in some way affecting the guests and vice versa. Therefore, guests are going to be the final decision-makers in the long run.

From the looks of it, hotels are planning to introduce automated systems to reduce the cost of manpower while charging pre-Covid rates to customers. This is a classic example of passing the blow on to the consumers and the staff while saving themselves. We've very recently seen the effect of guests on the hospitality industry. Therefore, hotels might need to be slightly more careful in their interactions. And although the idea of minimising contact is revolutionary (keeping Covid-19 in mind), monetising the same with the intention of keeping your own pockets full while letting the guests and staff suffer might just be killing the golden goose.

Will Domestic Travellers Boost India's Tourism Sector?

There was a time when Indians took pride in travelling to foreign locales and swapped stories with their friends on what exotic destinations they'd holidayed in. However, post-pandemic travellers are happy to just be out of the confines of their home, and local destinations are a safe bet. Could this lead to the revival of the Indian tourism sector? I hope so...

The contribution that domestic travel makes to the growth of the tourism and hospitality sectors in India has been a topic of discussion for quite a few years now. In recent years, we have seen domestic travel pique the interest of both government and public sector stakeholders and receive substantial support through various schemes. Some examples are PRASAD (Pilgrimage Rejuvenation and Spiritual Augmentation Drive), Swadesh Darshan for infrastructure development, UDAN for better air connectivity, and IRCTC (Indian Railways Catering and Tourism Corporation) launching travel packages to promote domestic travel. The domestic sector reached an annual growth rate of 25.3% in 2019, growing almost nine-fold since 2000.

The expectations from 2020 were very high until the turbulence caused by the pandemic pushed the entire industry to a record low. But even after the great pause caused by lockdowns and travel restrictions, the hospitality and tourism industries are looking at domestic tourism as the driver of recovery. Will native travellers be the boost the sectors need? Only time will tell! But the signs look very positive...

Domestic Travellers Will Rise and Shine

Going back to the statistics of 2019, domestic travel spending had contributed 83% to the total income of the hospitality sector. This share was primarily driven by the increased disposable income of the working middle class. Pressured for leisure time, they opted to travel to nearby or easily accessible destinations on long weekends or summer vacations. The pandemic forced people to alter their working patterns and routines and stay confined to their homes. This has triggered a desire to step out and travel to a destination that offers a change from their now-usual environment. With companies offering the flexibility to work remotely, travellers do not have the restrictions of time or days while considering a trip to a nearby or faraway destination, as long as they can remain connected.

The Year of Domestic Tourism in India

While 2020 was excruciating for hospitality and travel businesses, the sector has been slowly limping its way up. The demand for leisure travel has not entirely diminished, and as soon as the travel restrictions were relaxed, most destinations at drivable distances from cities saw travellers arrive. A survey by booking.com shows that 67% of the total distance travelled by Indians between June 1 and August 31, 2020, was within the country, compared to only 34% during the same period of 2019.

Domestic travel started peaking from 2021, with a huge diversion from outbound travel to travelling within the country. A survey revealed that 51% of Indians living in urban areas preferred a domestic vacation. To top that, approximately 40 million outbound travellers from India chose to travel domestically. This helped in increasing the market size of domestic tourism in the country. Throughout the pandemic era, the Dekho Apna Desh initiative (Explore India) by the Ministry of Tourism helped create awareness about domestic destinations.

Hospitality Will Be a Part of the Glory

The rise of domestic tourism has also helped in the growth of the intertwined hotel industry. Based on the Federation of Hotel and Restaurant Association of India (FHRAI) 2017–18 survey, the share of domestic guests for all the hotels across India was a soaring 77.3%, with an average stay of 2.5 days. In FY 2020, 23321.98 million people travelled within the country. The upward trend of domestic travel spending is projected to rise by 7.8% per annum to 13,305.5 billion in 2026. From a soaring success to struggling to survive, the sector was largely impacted by lockdowns and the travel restrictions in 2020.

However, it was also the first segment to see the light of hope once the lockdowns were relaxed. Although very miniscule as compared to the previous years, hotels across the country have received some business through domestic travellers. There has been a slow growth in occupancy rates from 23% in August 2020 to 36.4% in November 2020. The increase of the average rate per room (from ₹3,498.04 to 4,232.57) and the revenues earned per room (INR805.34 to 1,540.21) during this period is a good sign as well.

The existing infrastructure in India is already well-equipped to cater to a large segment of domestic travellers. Of the 1,05,344 rooms available in 1,423 approved hotels under the Ministry of Tourism, an approximate 95% fall in the low-priced bracket that is affordable for an average domestic traveller. Another interesting figure that caught our attention is that in 2019, 83% of Airbnb guests in India were domestic travellers. The online accommodation platform alone has more than 55,000 listings in the country. The past statistics look very optimistic when talking about how domestic tourism can facilitate the upturn of the tourism sector and every other ancillary services sector that it engages.

While the organised travel segment of domestic tourism is yet to find its foot back in the game, the hospitality industry has innovated itself. The emerging new concepts of workcation, work from hotel, pod travel, and the new buzzword, 'revenge travel', are encouraging long-haul travel and will hopefully increase the average stay duration to a minimum of five to seven days in the near future.

Domestic travel holds immense potential to boost the recovery of hospitality and tourism going forward. The stakeholders and various associations have been very persuasive on the subject ever since the pandemic brought the industry to a standstill. Despite the pertinent efforts, numerous requests and recommendations, the budgetary allocations for the Ministry of Tourism for FY 2021–22 were extremely disappointing. The hopes of support from the central government were shattered when the allocations were cut down by 19%. However, native travellers' growing desire to explore and experience a destination will help the sector to sustain itself. We will see destinations and hotels rediscovering themselves and innovating concepts to attract travellers their way. Domestic tourism is definitely here to stay.

"Work only a half a day; it makes no difference which half-it can be either the first 12 hours or the last 12 hours."

– Kemmons Wilson's (Holiday Inn)

The pandemic has made visionaries out of hoteliers. In generating new revenue streams due to the losses incurred, hoteliers have begun a new trend—Work from Hotels (WFH). A hip solution for travellers that started with big hotel chains has now been extended to lavish resorts and aims to provide an amenities-studded remote working environment.

The lockdown was unkind to the tourism and hospitality industry. Almost all the major events of 2020 that included one form or another of travel or stays were cancelled. There was a travel ban in place that resulted in almost no travel from one place to another—locally, nationally, or internationally. As a result, the Indian tourism industry had to face an insurmountable loss of revenue and livelihood.

However, while hotels were being reduced to quarantined areas, some hoteliers got creative and started looking for ways to develop new business lines. Food delivery from hotel restaurants, chef cooking sessions on demand, and premium laundry services were the result of such innovations. Hotels were still struggling to stop their revenue drops when they initiated another interesting concept to serve the travellers' community—work from hotels.

Work from Hotels

Some smart and farsighted hoteliers suggested the start of a new WFH trend—work from hotels. Differing from working vacations, *or workcations as Gen Z likes to call it,* the new work-from-hotels trend was targeted towards working individuals who were displaced by the pandemic. A large section of people, including students, professionals, and co-working start-ups were in desperate need of a place to stay and work, and this requirement was soon converted into a smart win-win situation for both parties thanks to the workstations provided by hotels.

Tapping into this growing potential, hotels have started letting out their premises, providing a safe, alternative working space to individuals and organisations looking to work from remote locations. Plush, comfy, and surprisingly cost-effective, these spaces are coming up in some of the best hotels around the country. Hotels like the Westin, Gurgaon, have been receiving enquiries from start-ups and companies that have given up their offices and now seek flexibility for their workspaces. And thus, we have quite a few hotels acting as working spaces right now.

Amenities

Hotels are providing trendy, vibrant workspaces that fuel productivity and innovation in the teams while still adhering to the authorities' safety and hygiene protocols. Hotel rooms are available for rent on a daily basis to corporates, businesses, and small-scale start-ups. In some places, it includes a private outdoor patio and floor-to-ceiling windows, while in others, people have to be satisfied with free beverages. The range of amenities varies from hotel to hotel. However, strong Wi-Fi connections and no-disturbance private meeting spaces are included in almost all workcations.

Hotels have constantly been receiving requests from corporate clients regarding their stays and offices. And most of these requests come with a demand for a personalised hotel space according to the client's needs. Hotels have thus started architecturally restructuring their premises to accommodate this work culture. Be it a request for banquet halls, suites, common areas with desks, or even the admittance of pets on the premises, hoteliers are ready to accommodate most of their clients' requests.

Recent Developments

The Westin in Gurgaon, New Delhi, recently announced the launch of its premium luxury co-working spaces at the hotel premises. The 25,000 sq. ft. of co-working space is provided with all-inclusive amenities, including specially curated meals and snack boxes delivered straight to the desks.

From economy to luxury hotel chains, such as Ibis, Novotel, and Sarovar, they have ventured into co-working spaces, offering businesses and start-ups a safe and cost-effective working area.

The Taj Mahal Palace in Mumbai is also providing premium services to companies. It has multiple state-of-the-art business centres, which are available for guests and companies.

Work from Resorts

One such interesting venture can be seen in Kolkata, where WFH has been further upgraded to 'Work From Resorts', with resorts like Ambuja Neotia Hospitality, Ibiza: The Fern Resort & Spa, Breathing Earth Resort, and Raajkutir Swabhumi providing workcation premises to their guests. Boutique hotels and resorts have introduced their Covid-specific packages for professionals seeking luxury and lavish experiences along with the ease of working. Besides, the inclusion of various amenities has not brought down the resorts' safety standard by even a bit, with fully functional and well-equipped sanitised rooms, indoor activities, and on-premise entertainment areas.

Hotels have been catering to business guests for a very long time now. Corporate meetings, business trips, overseas pitching, and on-site work for employees have all been accommodated by the hotels themselves. But as the entire office premises (at least for small start-ups) shift to hotels, it gives rise to a new and promising trend. For smart hoteliers, though, workcation is an interesting proposal. On the one hand, they have the opportunity to boost their low occupancy rates while on the other, they can have an upgrade in convenience, safety, and productivity for their guests, something that's going to stay for the long term. It is heartening to note that even today, the work-from-home concept continues and has become the new normal for many executives and corporates.

The Four Pillars that Will Strengthen Hotels' Guest Experience

There's no denying that the pandemic has changed the way travellers think, which in turn has affected the demands they're making on hotels. How can you cater to them? How can you ensure that you tick all the boxes?

As the travel and hospitality industries are on the path to restarting after months of unprecedented standstill, ensuring a seamless traveller experience will be even more crucial for hotels. It is obvious that the diaspora of travel behaviour across the world has changed. The stress travellers have experienced because of uncertainties, cancellations, and unclear refund policies in the wake of the pandemic was immense. They will now be even more careful about their choices. They will have a greater understanding of their travel needs and seek out hotels that can match or exceed their specific service expectations. At the first hint of a bad experience, they might even leave a brand they've been loyal to for years.

You probably understand by now that in the post-pandemic travel era, cleanliness, health, and safety will take the front seat. But as a hotelier, you have to be mindful of the untold expectations as the slightest miss would take your customer loyalty and branding downhill. The guest experience that you provide will be a turning point for your hotel in the new era of hospitality.

How can you take your hotel's guest experience up by a notch?

Customers Are Your First Priority

While there are a lot of variables that will now impact people's travel decisions, tending to their convenience will set you apart from the others. You have to be extra flexible in your policies to convey that you are considerate of their concerns. Travellers will prefer to book a hotel that is ready to accommodate their requirements. Clearly communicating about the ease of choosing you will bring traffic to your side.

For example, it may seem that you are losing out on your revenues by not relaxing charges on last-minute cancellations, but in the long run, this will reap you benefits. You will be able to retain the trust of your customers and can count on word-of-mouth publicity and referral business coming your way, too.

Customer Experience Will Be More than Just Services

The pandemic has influenced the customer service dynamics in a great way. Quick delivery of services, transparency to your policies, and immediate feedback are inevitable changes. You have to adjust your hotel's processes to swiftly resolve issues, especially when it comes to cancellations and refunds. You will have to be conscious that customers will no longer be adherent to discrepancies in your policies. A study by Microsoft reported that for 96% of consumers, customer service plays a significant role in their choice of loyalty to a brand. While the statistics are not exclusive to the hospitality industry, the higher percentage clearly indicates that customer experience is pivotal to the decision-making process.

But what will play a very important role in customer experience is making it more humane. If a situation or query requires more time to resolve, ensure that your customer service team tends to them with an acknowledgement and provide them with a tentative timeline if possible. At the same time, being mechanical in your communications will backfire. Care and empathy towards your customers will help you gain and strengthen their loyalty to you.

Everyone Is a Competition for You

You are not just in competition with another hotel on your service standards. The benchmark of expectations will be based on every service that the customers have experienced. Even if it is outside the hospitality industry, customers will compare their experiences of buying a product to staying at your hotel. If you are unaware or reluctant to deliver to those standards, it could become a reason for both new as well as long-standing customers to switch from your hotel. This will negatively impact customers' loyalty and the goodwill of your hotel in the long run.

Apart from customer experience, you will most likely face competition from high-end hotels, who are willing to bring down their tariff to a lower price bracket to attract your segment of customers. Retaining customers loyal to your brand may become all the more important. While you may not be able to compete with these ghost competitors, adding a recall value to your services will help you influence customers to take the final call in your favour.

Focus on Gaining Customer Loyalty

Customer loyalty is a direct, positive impact of the high-quality customer experience that you provide. Retaining an existing customer will cost you at least 6x times less than attracting a new one. Additionally, your brand patrons are 5x times more likely to re-purchase a product or service and 4x times more likely to send a recommendation to a friend. The ripple effect is just what you might be looking for.

In the post-Covid era of hospitality, people are ready to spend an extra amount for the desired services but may also shift to a different hotel if your hotel doesn't meet their expectations. It is understandable if you are focusing your efforts on procuring bookings at this stage. But you also have to focus on the post-booking experiences to ensure customer retention. Once a booking is confirmed, and you have the customer details in your database, follow up with a personalised note that says you are waiting to serve them. You can also take a survey of their preferences and prepare for their arrival with customised services.

However, the most important aspect is to provide excellent services while they are in-house. There is no comparison to in-person human interaction, but given the times, you have to tread carefully. Respecting their privacy while also making them feel safe, you have to ensure that guests have the best experience when staying in the property. Tending to in-room requests, you have to ensure that your delivery is impeccable, with minimum turnover time. Irrespective of your occupancy rate of the day, your staff should be equipped to pay extra attention to every customer so that their loyalty is embedded with your brand.

The pandemic has affected people at individual and organisational levels; recovering from the setback will require time and extreme patience. Travellers will slowly start trusting service providers again. But to ensure that, hotels will have to consciously and continuously work towards sustaining the faith that customers have in them. Your post-pandemic customer service policies will have to evolve from what it was before. First, by recognising the deficits, and second, by implementing processes to reverse them. You can start by sending out surveys to your existing, especially repeat, clientele to understand their expectations. One step at a time, you will have to be ready for the new language of customer experience and customer satisfaction.

"Pay attention to the big themes because that's what will
help you earn ten times your money."

– Barry Sternlicht (Starwood Hotels)

Could Wellness Tourism Provide the Boost the Hospitality Industry Needs?

Post Covid-19 and after travel norms have been relaxed, it almost feels like the only natural thing for people to do would be to seek out wellness-related initiatives. And it's quite possible that this desire to put the pandemic behind us could be the impetus the hospitality industry needs to get back on its feet.

Covid 19, made the world slowdown in unexpected ways. The hospitality industry took the biggest hit, dropping to an all-time low in business. The industry recovered bravely after the launch of coronavirus vaccines and the strict initiatives taken by governments worldwide.

However, the pandemic had a paradigm impact on traveller behaviour across the world. It instilled a strong sense of responsibility towards one's personal, physical, and mental well-being. This understanding definitely influenced travellers' choices of destinations and experiences. Moreover, with the world turning to healthier lifestyles, wellness tourism holds great promise of restoring the hotel industry in the coming year.

Why Wellness Tourism?

Wellness tourism has already been in high demand in recent years. Growing disposable incomes and affordable long-haul flights have made wellness destinations far more accessible to the global middle class. New-age travellers do not just want to tick their boxes with monuments and sightseeing anymore. They seek immersive experiences and ways to unwind, relax, and learn something new while they are on vacation. Experiential travel preferences and a deep-rooted desire to lead a healthy lifestyle have paved the way for wellness tourism to thrive. With the pandemic forcing travellers worldwide to stay homebound for months at a stretch, people are no longer looking for a fancy hotel with modern amenities. Even the most generic tourist is likely to participate in a wellness experience that the hotel has to offer.

The Wellness Tourism Market

In its initial phases, wellness tourism was a niche product targeted to premium-spending travellers only. However, in 2018, an economic report by the Global Wellness Institute revealed some very encouraging numbers. The report noted that the wellness tourism economy had one of the highest growth rates at 6.7% in the tourism segment, which is twice the annual growth rate of general tourism. It accounted that on average, an international tourist spent 53% more and a domestic tourist spent 178% more as compared to what a general tourist spent. The report also projected that wellness tourism will amount to 1.2 billion trips in 2022.

As countries across the globe relaxed their travel restrictions, a trend of domestic travellers seeking immersive experiences emerged. Despite the worldwide crisis, wellness tourism in 2020 was estimated at USD 735.8 billion!

Wellness Tourism and India

The fast-growing wellness segment already has a strong foothold in mainstream Indian tourism. We are among the top 10 wellness tourism destination markets in the world with an average annual growth of 20.3% (2015–17). Kerala, for example, has been positioning itself in the wellness tourism market as the 'Land of Ayurveda' for over two decades now, promoting wellness-based

tourism experiences in destinations. Properties in the Himalayas have also capitalised on the segment by branding themselves as specialised retreats for yoga, meditation, and ayurvedic health. In cities, luxury business hotels and boutique resorts, too, have incorporated features in their properties to grasp a section of the earnings generated by wellness tourism. From airport spas tapping the market of travellers in transit to restaurants serving health-focused specialty cuisines, wellness tourism has opened avenues for every business in the hospitality industry even before the world was hit by the pandemic.

Will You Have to Change Everything?

While established wellness retreats will have an advantage in the bounce-back phase because they already have the set-ups to serve this segment of tourists, the rest of the hospitality industry will also be able to reap the benefits. You can fit wellness features into your existing infrastructure by adjusting your hotel's offerings. Repurpose room appearances with sustainability features, add amenities to promote better sleep, and find ways for noise cancellation in the rooms if you are not already doing so. If you have the space, consider engaging an expert to lead meditation and yoga sessions or collaborate with a specialised wellness consultant. Curate menus and culinary experiences that focus on health and well-being.

The Way Forward

Stringent hygiene standards, privacy, and minimum contact services have been a priority always and will remain an increasingly essential inclusion in guest experience in the post-pandemic travel era. Hotels will have to embrace the boon of technology to provide engaging yet safe experiences to guests. It could be as complex as installing an aromatherapy diffuser to as simple as encouraging guests to brew a traditional detox drink with the ingredients and recipe you have placed in their room. The idea is to identify and incorporate elements that will set you apart from your competitors.

It is important for hoteliers to identify your hotel's strengths in the wellness segment. Not only should you focus on the features you can offer or enhance, but in doing so, you should also be mindful of the target audience you are fully capable of catering to. An experience, no matter how small, must be holistic and backed by incomparable services. This will create goodwill amongst the targeted consumers, and in the long run, build brand value for your hotel as well.

The tourism and hospitality industries have revived and are on an upward trend. With the *Federation of Indian Chambers of Commerce and Industry (FICCI)* advocating for an all-new category of visas for ayurveda and wellness tourism, the future of wellness tourism in India looks very promising. We have seen hotels innovate, reinvent, and sustain themselves in a time of global crisis. What comes next is finding newer ways to flourish!

"The men and women of Accor have Inherited a unique cultural legacy: the sense of hospitality, the unfailing ability to anticipate and meet the needs of their guests with genuine attention to detail."

– Paul Dubrule/Gerard Pellisson (Novotel)

Is Airbnb Showing Hotels the Way Again? How to Bounce Back from the Pandemic

In the wake of the Covid-19 pandemic, the hospitality industry was one of the worst affected sectors. Amidst the gloom, Airbnb rose to the top, utilising its expertise and swiftly transforming itself to make the best out of the present-day travel scenario. From refunding bookings amounts to offering experiences online, they have been able to engage and retain their two primary stakeholders—guests and hosts. The hospitality industry can learn a lot from Airbnb on how to win the battle against Covid-19.

A little over a decade after its launch, Airbnb has now become a prominent name in the hospitality industry. With a business model that connects travellers directly to the community, the company redefined travel experiences around the globe. Over the years, it has also contributed to the communities by launching remarkable campaigns of help and support in times of distress. Encouraging hosts to open up their homes free during natural disasters like Hurricane Sandy (2012) or the Nepal earthquake (2015); supporting people affected by the Pulse nightclub shooting (2016); launching a medical stays initiative (2018); or offering frontline stays to Covid-19 first responders.

From facing an existential crisis during the pandemic to a remarkable comeback, Airbnb is a significant story of resilience and recovery. It has responded to the pandemic relatively well as compared to other service providers. Leaders of the hospitality industry can certainly take some pointers from Airbnb on how to bounce back from the pandemic.

Monitor Trends, Assess Changes, and Adapt Quickly

In the wake of the pandemic, countries worldwide imposed travel restrictions and banned international flights. Airbnb not only assessed the situation rightly, but was also the first few to create awareness about the risks of travelling during the pandemic. Furthermore, it collaborated with medical experts to develop an Enhanced Cleaning Protocol for their hosts.

But the impact of the pandemic was as severe on them as any other company in the travel or hospitality industry. As the lockdowns relaxed, Airbnb's site noticed an upward trend in searches for nearby suburban and rural locations. This was a positive aspect that it did not let go of. In June 2020, it revamped its website in a matter of days. It removed all international flights, in-person experiences, and cross-border travel and instead focused on domestic travel, highlighting stays within a shorter radius from cities and long-term stays. It encouraged hosts to accept bookings for long-term stays along with flexible policies. The result? As compared to just 52% in January 2020, Airbnb's domestic business increased to 77% by September 2020 in India.

Find Solutions without Losing Focus on the Core Philosophy of Your Business

Airbnb calls itself a 'community based on connection and belonging'. Over the years, it has introduced travellers to communities in remote locations, away from mainstream travel destinations. In a shareholders' letter, the founders noted that when the pandemic hit, they knew that, moving forward, they would have to focus on what is unique about Airbnb. It returned to its roots—the everyday people who welcome travellers to their homes and provide local experiences and an insider's view of a community so that the guests feel like locals rather than tourists.

So, it scaled back investments that did not directly support the core of their host communities.

When in-person experiences were no longer an option amidst the upsurge of the pandemic, Airbnb introduced online experiences. Taking advantage of its existing user base, it brought in an array of activities from various parts of the world to people's living rooms. From cooking classes to guided meditation, what otherwise was suggested as an add-on only to travellers in person became accessible to a much larger audience. Allowing free Zoom access to the hosts, Airbnb now has more than 100 hosts from over 30 countries who are bringing their unique experiences online. With virtual experiences like a visit to an animal sanctuary or field trips for parents to support after-school learning, Airbnb has enabled the global community to *find unique activities led by one-of-a-kind hosts—all without leaving home.*

Hoteliers should definitely learn about preserving the human connection with Airbnb's strategy of bringing hosts and community stories to the forefront. Collaborating with local communities, Airbnb continues to promote travel experiences virtually. Going online with experiences has generated revenue for both Airbnb and the host community. A month after the launch of online experiences, Airbnb saw a 3x increase in bookings from India alone. Globally, the market value of Airbnb has been boosted by more than 300% in nine months despite the disruptions by the pandemic.

Effective Communication is Imperative

While communicating about a crisis can be challenging, it is what sets you apart from your competitors. Instead of just stating facts, Airbnb chose to make its messages more humane, conveying empathy and standing in solidarity with the industry. Its refund policies, while a boon for travellers, faced a huge backlash from hosts, and to address them, Airbnb set up a newsroom, which provided detailed information about the initiatives it undertook to support their hosts; it continues to provide regular updates on their Covid-related policies. Right from the beginning of the Covid-19 crisis, it involved the top management in its messaging, including CEO Brian Chesky's detailed_letter when it decided to let go of a quarter of its workforce in May 2020.

Maintaining transparency in communications, Airbnb has been able to retain the trust of their user base as well. While it may not be possible for individual hotels to match the range of Airbnb's communication strategies, hoteliers should focus on creating engaging content instead of posting only your hotels' amenities. You could tell a heartfelt story of a staff member, a chauffeur, or a local guide who has contributed towards making a guest's experience memorable or how your hotel went the extra mile to facilitate a request from a guest in the past. Put out regular updates on how you fared during the pandemic or how you reviewed your operating protocols and cleanliness guidelines and updated guests' policies. Share your hotel's stories of dealing with the pandemic or how you prepared for recovery. However, while doing so, be mindful that your message is empathetic and humane and not mechanised or self-serving. The idea is to stay visible as well as memorable ensuring that your guests feel connected and reassured.

So, What is the Final Takeaway for Hoteliers?

The year 2020 was anticipated to be another milestone for Airbnb, with the company deciding to go public. However, the unprecedented outbreak of the Covid-19 pandemic affected its rapid pace, as it did the rest of the hospitality and travel industry. With the market going on a standstill for months, Airbnb's revenues dropped by 80% in March 2020. Facing the hard truth of its business falling apart, it initiated cost-cutting measures—25% of its workforce was laid off, executive salaries were lowered, and all capital expenditures were halted. Every building block of the company was hit by the pandemic. With the company's market value plunging by 24%, many would have assumed that the pandemic ended Airbnb's success run. However, Airbnb quickly adapted to the changes, recreated itself, and reintroduced itself to millions of people. On December 10, 2020, it went public with a $47 billion valuation, which is the largest travel IPO debut ever.

From the brink of collapse at the onset of the pandemic to the largest travel IPO debut, Airbnb adapted, evolved, and transformed itself. With strategic agility, it has once again positioned itself very well in an extremely dynamic market. It leveraged its strength in the digital space, acted swiftly, and restructured its offerings. It ensured that it remained true to its philosophy—probably the only significant change that happened was that the experiences became virtual.

"Why not put a hotel next to all the big airports
so that a traveller need never worry about missing a plane,
and would have somewhere to sleep
at the end of a long journey?"

– Jay Pritzker (Hyatt)

Workspitality: A New Trend that is Helping Hotels Reinvent Themselves

For working professionals, the lines between work and home have become blurred as several companies have passed the work-from-home mandate, which continues even today. However, a new trend of taking work-from-hotel vacations (workcations) brings relief and inspiration not only to travellers but also to the hospitality industry.

The idea of being able to catch up on work while being on holiday is not a new concept, but it was usually limited to a few highly ambitious and workaholic professionals. What was referred to as a *workliday* at the beginning of this decade has now been catalysed by the pandemic, snowballed by the crisis, and rechristened as a *workation or workcation.*

However, if you look further back, creative minds of all times have chosen to move away from the hustle and bustle of society to reflect on ideas, find artistic inspiration, or delve into their mind palaces. Rabindranath Tagore penned down parts of his Nobel Prize-winning *Gitanjali* while staying in a holiday home in Uttarakhand. Rudyard Kipling and Ruskin Bond found their calling in the foothills of the Himalayas. Even the Beatles took the path of self-discovery away from the confines of their homes. It may not have been a trend then, but it is our innate nature to find solace and motivation from outside.

What Workcations Mean in the Pandemic Era

While change is inevitable, the shift imposed by the pandemic has startled the entire world. Amid the prevailing negatives that have engulfed our lives, it has become challenging to stay driven, maintain productivity, and achieve the same levels of efficiency as before.

Workcations are a boon for those who work remotely but are starting to show signs of fatigue. Switching to the comforts of a much more pleasant environment, where health and safety is not a concern, yet being able to continue working without interruptions, is definitely a welcome change. Once, such an option would have been far-fetched; now it is an option offered by more and more hotels across the board.

With these new developments, the traditional marketing strategies of the hospitality and travel industry may no longer apply for a while. For starters, the seasonal nature of travel has more or less perished. If the main aim is to work from a scenic location, people aren't going to be too fussed about peak season or off seasons. Similarly, holiday or weekend-oriented approaches are fading, too, with people looking at long-term workcation options.

But, instead of being daunted by these changes, hoteliers should look at this as a dream opportunity they never had before. While business or leisure travel may have been the major sources of revenue generation for you in the pre-pandemic era, workcations are what you should look at to get you back on your feet. Think of long-haul stays, minimum interaction, marginal utilisation of resources, and higher revenues.

Hospitality to Workspitality: A Changing Dynamic

The pandemic has changed life as we knew it. Although we keenly observed how the situation developed when it came to international travel, when Indian states relaxed their policies, domestic travellers cautiously started stepping out of their homes.

Adapting to the needs of these guests, major brands and boutique hotels alike have adjusted their operations—offering staycation or daycation packages and allowing them to break the months of monotonous work-from-home regime. High-speed internet, power backup, and a designated work desk are the bare essentials that a traveller looks for during a workcation. Privacy, cleanliness, and stringent health, safety, and hygiene protocols are of course critical. A few adjustments to the existing amenities and service policies have certainly helped hoteliers to appeal to this new clientele that has emerged from the ripple effects of the pandemic.

A Little Something for Everybody

The spectrum of workspitality is not just limited to individuals seeking a retreat from an unexciting work-from-home regime. With more than one family member caught in this involuntary arrangement, a planned workcation is a way to spend quality time with loved ones despite the adversities of recent times. Facilitating the routine of everyday office work with the conveniences of a professional environment while providing safe and interesting activities to individuals or a group of travellers is like getting two giggles from one tickle!

In a prediction for the upcoming months, booking.com estimates that workcations will not be limited to a couple of days but are likely to extend over weeks or months. And travellers will look at not just retreats located at drivable distances from their cities: they will also set off further to offbeat locations. Working remotely from a remote location.

Although a high-speed internet connection is the most sought-after amenity for a workcation, it is no longer just limited to that. Travellers are also looking for packages that encompass other components of a vacation. There is a lot that hoteliers could experiment with. It can be an alfresco spread for lunch or a simple walking trail in the vicinity of the property for short breaks between work. Curated experiences to engage kids while the grown-ups are set for the workday or special weekend activities like hiking and camping. If your hotel serves cuisine unique to the region, you can encourage your guests to learn a local recipe. For the wellness enthusiast, yoga and meditation sessions would work very well. Travellers will be looking for various ways to reconnect with nature, with loved ones, and with themselves, so hotels will have to reinvent their rejuvenation quotient away from the regular spa and massage therapies. Keeping safe distance in mind, workcationers will also look to forming better lifestyle habits, boosting immunity, and unwinding, all while maintaining their regular work schedules.

Village homestays, boutique hotels, wildlife lodges, and wellness retreats do have an edge as their existing infrastructure resonates with the workcation requirements that travellers seek. They are spread out and have limited occupancy and quieter surroundings. As a hotelier, you have to be mindful of what you lay on the table and how you put the word out. It is also important to assess the local social and natural environment you are in and evaluate the results of vacationers' visits. Being **sensitive** to the needs of the traveller, ensuring the **safety** of guests and staff alike, and implementing **sustainable** operational practices will be crucial going forward.

This makeshift option of offering workcations has the potential to convert from temporary occupancies to a more permanent travel classification altogether—tailoring the existing experiences by aligning the norms of the present settings with high standards of services/amenities. To gain the confidence of prospective travellers, hotels should start offering transparent and flexible terms of bookings, modifications, and cancellations. Add-ons—such as the availability of a health care provider in case of emergencies, insurance coverage, elderly care facilities, and pet-friendly solutions—for the duration of stay will encourage a broader segment of workcationers to choose a retreat.

With survival instincts kicking in, the hotel industry has been able to diversify their offerings, whether it be city hotels repurposing their spaces to cater to working professionals or curating safe experiences most effective to their specific destinations. While 2020 may be a year the entire hospitality industry would like to happily leave behind, there are lessons that can be learnt from the crisis going ahead. It is important that hoteliers anticipate the needs of potential guests and strategise their marketing campaigns accordingly. Stringent housekeeping protocols and the health and well-being of the staff will have to be a priority, and flexibility to meet the requirements of travellers will play an important role in sustaining business.

While it will be difficult for gadgets to match human interaction, it will be interesting to see how contactless services will be developed to convey the warmth of personalised hospitality. Innovation and sensibility will have to go hand in hand. Hoteliers have to be cautious about their offers and messaging as an attractive discount will not be the only criteria travellers will look for. A combination of meaningful experiences, along with privacy and a work-friendly set-up, is the way to go forward.

"You can make a hotel of pure gold, but no-one will visit unless you provide quality service"

– Biki Oberoi (Oberoi Hotels and resorts)

An Ideal Hotel Amid Covid-19: Robots, IoT, and No-Contact Solutions

The hotel industry has always been driven by human interactions—the warmth of a greeting, the charm of a smile extended to travellers, and the instinctive desire to help them with any problems they may have. But the novel Coronavirus changed everything, and now, hotels are having to rely on technological interventions to make guests feel not just welcome but also safe.

Due to the widespread pandemic that the world experienced, many industries faced what could be described as the toughest time in their existence. The worst affected among them was the tourism and hospitality industry, which saw losses of $1.2 trillion in 2020. This loss in revenue made it very difficult to maintain hotel properties and attract customers, even after the lifting of travel restrictions. In an attempt to earn people's trust, hotel owners are speeding up their process of integrating technology into the hospitality industry. They are also prioritising the usage of all the things that people are going to trust in these testing times—robots, smart solutions, and completely contactless service.

For generations now, the hospitality industry has been based on human interactions. Replacing that with a complete boycott of human touch is unlikely to be seamless. However, hotels will have to look for smarter and more trustworthy ways of delivering services to earn the trust of their customers. And one of the best ways to do this is with the help of machines. Because of machines, a lot of technological solutions are now lined up for big hotel chains to adopt. From digital tracking and monitoring to a complete touchless technological experience, let's see how all of these solutions are going to affect our hotel experiences in the upcoming years and turn hotels into smart hotels.

Robots as Concierge, Butlers, and Cleaning Assistants

Though the pandemic might have sped up the rate at which hotels are integrating technology into their experience, it wasn't completely unheard of even before. Many big and innovative groups had already been planning technological interventions in the hospitality industry, and thus, have a solution ready to be used and deployed.

Managed by the Alibaba Future Hotel group, the Alibaba Flyzoo Hotel in China was looking at robotic and humane hospitality experiences back in 2018. The 290-'smart' room hotel relies heavily on robotic assistance—from concierges to room service to even bars! And while people may take their time adjusting to a robot that delivers their drinks, this experience will definitely help them trust hotels in these testing times.

Robots are also being used as cleaning assistants in many hotels. Helsinki-based Valpas uses robotic assistance to get rid of bedbugs, taking cleaning to a whole new level. Some hotels are switching to robots with inbuilt UV-ray cleaning systems. And so confident are they of their UV cleaning robots, they claim you can lick the TV remote in a room after it is cleaned by a UV robot.

Hotels, Smart Solutions, and the Internet of Things

Privacy concerns aside, hotel-integrated artificial intelligence can now provide a solution to people's hesitation to touch surfaces. Taking their help from the Internet of Things (IoT), hotels are now equipping their customers with smart devices, which can do almost everything traditional room service can.

From ordering food to opening curtains, inbuilt smart devices can help with high-end features like cross-property integration and management between different branches. At the same time, they're also able to help with smaller tasks, such as calling an elevator to the floor you're on.

'Smart' guest room management systems are often used in many different hotels as a solution to hotel lighting controls, dynamic room configuration, and even thermostats. The system can detect the number of people in the room and regulate the thermostat accordingly. In addition, this wireless solution makes it easy for hotels to add switches and configure rooms without actually worrying about the physical wiring.

Automated Heat, Ventilation and Air-Conditioning (HVAC) systems are thus going to prove a major factor in a post-Covid hotel experience as they reduce the need for manual interventions to a great extent while optimising the existing systems.

A Contactless Hotel Experience

As technology advanced, hoteliers were keen on at least making their hotels look hi-tech, and they did so by placing interactive touchscreens at key locations in the property. However, these testing times demand that hotels move from touchscreens to completely automated voice and facial recognition, not to forget thermal sensing.

I spoke about the Alibaba Flyzoo Hotel in China as an example of one of the most innovative hotels right now. But what is especially impressive is their almost contactless service. This futuristic hotel contains no counters or couches in the hotel lobby, and you'd be forgiven for wondering if you've walked into the right address. Instead of the check-in counter, guests are documented using their facial data, which is used to access their hotel rooms and even their floors in an elevator! Fitness and recreational areas are also equipped with facial scans, making keycards and attendants a thing of the past.

This contactless service does not end there. With QR codes at every table at the restaurants, you can order and pay for the food online, which is, of course, delivered by a robotic waiter. Even the hotel vending machines and bars have their own QR codes, reducing the need for contact at almost every point.

The best part about all this technology is that it's driven by practicality. It maps the journey of the user through the property and identifies all the points of interaction that can be realistically replaced by a technological intervention. The other thing that fascinates me is that these robotics and AI-driven measures aren't just reserved for exquisite hotels in Saudi Arabia or luxury hotels in Europe. All these solutions will eventually come to hotels very close to you.

With smart solutions, robotic assistance, and contactless systems like these, hotels can be positive about bouncing back from the slump they've been in and winning back the trust of customers. However, though this looks like an effective solution, it is yet to be seen how people react to reduced human interaction in the long term. While hoteliers consider that going back from a robotic experience to traditional housekeeping techniques will be very tough, they're yet to know if customers respond well to a mechanical experience.

Hotels in the Pandemic: A Tale of Covid and Thinking Out of the Box

They say tough times call for tough measures. I believe that tough times demand that you rethink the way you've been doing business and come up with innovative ways to get yourself back on your feet. The hotel industry, especially, will have to do this in order to emerge from this pandemic and recover their losses.

As the world awaits an effective cure for Covid-19, businesses around the world continue to be affected. And while people have begun to feel comfortable working remotely, there are still many industries that depend heavily on human interaction for revenue generation, primarily the tourism and hospitality industry. Because of long periods of lockdowns and severe travel restrictions, most of the small tourism facilitators closed shop or hibernated, waiting for the right time to bounce back. Unfortunately, the same cannot be said for the hotel industry.

Our hotel industry relies upon, or relied till very recently, completely on the bookings done by an individual. However, due to the travel restrictions and fear, people are unwilling to travel to other places, thus amounting to almost no bookings. As a result, hotels have to start getting innovative, not just with the internal technical and sanitation aspects of the hotels but also with the modes of revenue, business renovating models, and marketing itself. And though travel has started at a slow and shaky pace post-October 2020, there's still a long way to go. Nevertheless, here are a couple of things hotels can do in addition to their already-in-process strategy.

Newer Revenue Streams

This is something that is already being practised by many big and small standalone hotels and hotel chains. As the lockdowns extended bit by bit, the hotels got creative, looking out for more revenue-generating streams. And this included big hotel chains with huge reserves, too.

While JW Marriott has started its own food delivery services (Marriott on Wheels), others like ITC have partnered up with food delivery services like Zomato and Swiggy, thus still remaining in touch with their customers.

Unlike several restaurants, hotels do not have to resort to selling groceries and essentials in their market areas. Hotels can remodel their vacant unutilised rooms to turn them into luxurious, socially distant restaurants. This will help their customers to recall the value of the brand and will also provide an additional revenue stream during these testing times.

Hotels can also rent out their rooms and lobbies as co-working spaces, generating more revenue. In addition, they can also help with the laundry services, bartender on call or even private chef services!

Reinvent Yourself

Tough times require tougher measures. Hotels need to set up a new standard for themselves. They need to change their working models and make their work both effective and smart. And what can help them to do this effectively is data, which is so easily available.

Data mining and usage are probably the most useful and effective growth methods in any industry today. And with the help of analytic tools and personnel, hoteliers, too, can gather relevant data and use it for various purposes. This includes the usage of data for feedback, targeted marketing, advertisements, and a lot of insight into the hospitality industry right now.

Hotels should start by hiring data analysts who are smart and can figure out at least a couple of steps ahead. Real-time chatbots and AIs on the websites of hotels could easily compile lists of grievances and hesitations that customers have. The data could also help hotels know where people are more satisfied with them and what they need to additionally work on.

However, the usage of data isn't the only way through which hotels can reinvent themselves. Hotels should reflect a bit on their policies regarding both guests and employees. Cancellations should be as lenient as possible (or at least seem so). Previous marketing trends have proved that coupons do really well. Thus, customers can have an option to redeem their cancellation at any other time.

Marketing Goes a Long Way

It was already difficult for businesses without able marketing strategies to survive in a cut-throat industry like hospitality. But with lockdowns and a lot of people depending upon advertisements as their source of information, marketing forms a huge chunk of the answer. This involves all forms of marketing, from brand marketing to public relations to direct marketing.

Staying in business during these times requires hotels to be in constant touch with their customers. They should thus make sure that they have enough visibility on enough platforms. This could be easily done with ads on social media. We know this is a difficult time the industry is going through, and many hoteliers would be hesitant to spend their reserves on marketing. However, if you look hard enough, you'll understand that marketing is something that's going to keep you alive for now.

Hoteliers should also tie up with local hospitals nearby, if possible. And market the same across all platforms. This will increase the reliability of the hotels and make customers way less hesitant. And among all of this, hotels should know better than to lose touch with their old customers. A simple personalised emailer can do wonders for an old customer.

As travel began slowly, demand for hotel stays rose again. However, hotels made sure that they had utilised the lockdown period in ways that would sustain even after the restrictions were lifted. Delivery services and tie-ups by big hotel chains continued even after the lockdown was over, they generated enough revenue during the period. Marketing budgets can continue in a similar manner, and the same goes for hotel policies— smarter and friendlier.

However, the efforts of the hotels must be visible to the people. When hotels reopened, it showed that they had taken their time to reinvent themselves, rather than pretending that everything was going to be the same once the pandemic was over.

In times of crisis, the first thing that companies tend to cut back on is their marketing budget. While this might save money in the short run, it could also delay the recovery of your hotel. So, relook at your decision to halt marketing and focus, instead, on making the strategy more relevant to current times.

While travel is on the rise in the post-pandemic period, isolated cases of outbreaks of Covid-19 variants in some parts of the globe make people sceptical about travelling again. Amid such testing times and such a huge loss of revenue, experts are recommending that hotels turn their attention to something that could be critical in recovering the major revenue loss—marketing.

The huge loss in revenue due to Covid-19 has already forced many small-scale service providers from these industries to close shop. Many big hotel chains, too, had to cut costs and resort to newer business lines to cope with the hit. In all this, asking hoteliers to pay attention towards an indirect revenue-generating activity like marketing seems like a far-fetched fantasy. However, if you look at it closely (and a bit differently), marketing can be a valuable opportunity in these times.

Using Digital Media to the Fullest

In almost every industry, cutting back on marketing spend is considered the easiest way to save money. In addition, with the huge hit that the hospitality industry has endured, coupled with the downward curve of the economy, hotels do not have a lot of money to run ads in magazines and newspapers or put up hoardings and billboards. A good alternative is using digital ads, which are not as expensive as traditional ads and have the potential to reach a larger and more qualified or targeted audience.

Another important thing a hotel should pay attention to is its social media content. Social media content does not require a significant outlay of money. However, it can bring in surprising results. As far as the content is concerned, hotels can start promoting their towns or countries, in addition to the hotel's ambience and facilities. Depending upon the section of audience they are targeting, hotels can direct their content to a regional, national, or international audience. A hotel should thus act as a tourism promoter by sharing photos of the destination rather than just sticking to hotel promotional methods.

In addition to the awesome content shared on their social media channel, hotels should also display their customer testimony, both from current and previous customers. This will help in validating the hotels and build trust among customers.

A hotel should also be active on other publicly accessible platforms like Google My Business, the hotel website, and customer care forums and be very prompt in replying to service reviews from customers.

Reassuring Guests

Because of social media, hotels have the perfect platform to stay in touch and reassure their guests. However, this is not the only way to get in touch with your customers. Hotels can, and should, contact their previous customers via emails, letting them know how safe their hotels actually are. They should start with the common questions of the audience. They should engage with customers and answer questions like, *'What kind of medical facilities are available for the guests'* or *'Are there still travel guidelines in the country, state, or the local administration?'* Basic questions like the documents required by the guests on their arrival are easy and will let them know that there is someone they can go to with their queries. These small, yet crucial, engagements will help hotels build trust and a two-way communication channel with customers, which will further result in organic conversions.

Internal Reflection

The COVID-19 crisis has left hotels gasping to consolidate their existing line of work and look out for the best and smartest ways to generate revenue. This is, thus, the best time to reflect on the working process of the company. Hotels need to market their USPs in front of the audience because the core of the hotel is something that is going to get them through this. In addition to the cleanliness protocols (that are mandatory for all hotels), hotels should market the one thing that makes them different. For some, it could be the proximity to a famous tourist destination while for some, it can

be the features of the hotels themselves. The hotel should reflect upon the one asset that gives it the best Return on Investment (ROI) and should market it.

Apart from all this, hotels should also make their booking processes smoother (like direct bookings) and bypass formalities wherever possible. They should also market the same on their social media handles to create awareness.

In any case, it should be kept in mind that while earlier marketing might just have been an attempt to stay in the race, right now, it is a revenue-generating stream.

Responding to Reviews

One of the most important aspects of marketing yourself is to address the reviews of your services. Guests do pick up on any short delivery of service. There are bound to be discrepancies, either in the booking process or in the services provided. Moreover, imperfect services will lead to grievances. Usually, hotels take care of reviews on a constant basis. However, at times, there can be an oversight in the review response section. This should be avoided because each negative review that is seen by hundreds of other people is going to decrease the probability of conversion exponentially.

A solution to this is to hire an Online Response Management (ORM) expert who takes care of the reviews, connects with the audience empathetically, and portrays the hotels as trusting and caring. In addition, this should be a regular practice not just in the comments sections of popular platforms like Facebook, Instagram, and X, but also on exclusive platforms like Trustpilot. Because sometimes, the exclusive platforms are the ones that customers believe the most.

Market Newer Business Lines

Since the pandemic, hotels have been exploring additional business lines. This has led to the creation of food delivery services, chef-at-home experiences, workcations, and many more that the hotels can still continue. Taking advantage of this, hotels should stress on marketing the additional services that started during the lockdown. However, they should only market those services that they plan to continue.

Digital marketing, in itself, is a converting revenue stream. Due to the wide audience reach in a short span, it can affect many people in a short time—something service calls cannot. However, due to a lesser number of conversions than through traditional means, digital marketing becomes the first to be cut off in the budget.

These times of chaos have made marketing one of the biggest ways to relate to an audience. Thus, they should not be scrapped completely. Even in a worst-case scenario, hotels should never let their marketing budget fall below 50% of what they were using before. Because if there is anything that hotels can bet on, it is marketing.

"I often compare putting a hotel together to old-time movie production. You come up with a story line, you hire the writer, the director, the stars, the set designer."

– André Balazs (André Balazs Properties)

Technology and Benchmarking: What is Expected of the Hospitality Industry?

Even before the pandemic, hotels were in the process of switching over to technologically robust measures and service offerings to cater to the 21st-century traveller. But with the novel coronavirus wreaking untold havoc on the world, hotels have discovered that technology might just be the saviour they need to pull them up from this slump

Thanks to Covid-19, hotels all over the world will remember 2020 as one of the least revenue-generating years ever. And true to the predictions of a few leading professionals across the globe, it took the industry over a year to recover and regain its stability.

Amid this chaos, hotels have begun to accept technology as their saviour. But is this just because of the pandemic?

There's no denying that the pandemic is going to transform the working of hotels, but it's also an undisputed fact that the hotel experience was already headed towards being dependent on technology. The pandemic has just pushed things along faster. And—I never thought I would say this—the need for technology to replace human contact has become imminent now. Furthermore, holistic technology strategies adopted by big hotel chains are setting a benchmark for other independent hotels to follow.

However, are these strategies equally useful for other lodging provisions like homestays and bed-and-breakfasts (B&Bs)?

How Are Big Hotel Chains Faring?

The big hotel chains that can afford certain technological strategies and measures are setting the industry standard for small independent hotels. Hotel chains like Hyatt have adopted innovative guest experiences like virtual meditation and rooftop yoga in an attempt to rope in people who are travelling. However, the primary marketing point of big hotel chains is their zero-contact experience. They're providing a social-distanced, touchless experience for cautious (and possibly sceptical) travellers while hoping that word of mouth will help carry the word to their fellow travellers and inspire confidence.

Some big hotel chains have also partnered with technology providers to make innovative solutions more accessible for travellers. The Indian Hotels Company Limited (IHCL) has launched contactless, technology-driven solutions for every guest touchpoint using QR codes and digital interventions—straight from check-ins to dine-ins. They have also installed thermal sensors and face recognition tech for their employees. To ensure that these efforts are visible to other travellers, hotels have talked about them in their communications on various digital platforms.

Sandals Resorts in Jamaica has taken a rather interesting approach to the crisis. It believes that after the primary requirements of health and safety are met, privacy is one luxury that people would definitely appreciate during their stay. Thus, it has taken efforts to make honeymoon suites as private and intimate as possible. It has also taken a similar approach for many VIP lounges.

While these measures are laudable, they're but the beginning of what hotels are doing to revive the business and instil confidence among travellers. And for this, big hotel chains are taking their digital presence to a whole new level.

Technology and Benchmarking

Breaking it down in the simplest of terms, big hotel chains are stressing their digital availability, sometimes as much as their services. During the period when travel was paused, big hotels increased their efforts to connect to most of their previous clients. Using technology not just for service providing but to increase brand value, these hotels know that any gesture that connects hotels with previous clients will be very much appreciated.

To that end, hotels have been integrating with the services of local hospitals. They have also kept their websites fresh and updated as required and use their blogs, emails, press releases, and social media posts to let their clients know that their hotels are safe, secure, and open.

Apart from this, hotels are targeting the right audience, staying up to date with market insights, and taking expert advice. With the help of technology, hotels are getting insights into the market's status and choosing the right demographics for promotion. This is keeping them current and prepared for any business challenge, and they're at the forefront of attracting as many guests as possible.

Pushing for More Business Lines

Along with the above precautions and measures, hotel chains are also using technology to embark on newer revenue streams. Smart marketers and a vast sea of technological resources have allowed hotel chains to provide people with food from in-house restaurants. IHCL, for example, has partnered up with Tata Digital for the Qmin app, which allows customers to personalise and track their deliveries in real time. This F&B offering is generating great revenue opportunities and brand recall value.

Are the Benchmarks the Same for All?

The market standards that big hotel chains are setting might be true for standalone hotels, but the same cannot be said for smaller homestays and B&Bs. Big brands and luxury hotel chains account for 1.4 lakh rooms, which accounts for just 5% of the total rooms available in India. The remaining 95% are B&Bs, guest houses, and very small hotels. And they need their own set of benchmarks.

Huge service providers like Airbnb have redesigned their products, focusing mainly on reviews of experiences and testimonies. However, even with enhanced cleaning protocols and a 24-hour vacancy between bookings, the homestay provider knows that now everyone is willing to travel. It has thus also been focusing on generating content for people to entertain themselves with. And from a revenue-generating prospect, it isn't completely idle either.

As hotel chains continue to set the trend with their technological advancements, it is certain that the technology is going to reach every one of us at one time or the other. And though it may not replace human contact as drastically as now, hotels will become heavily dependent on technology. Eventually, smaller hotels are going to adapt to the technological standards set by the big hotel chains. But how it fares for bed-and-breakfasts, is yet to be seen. Will B&Bs be willing to shed their emotion-first approach towards the customer and accept a technological solution? We'll have to wait and see.

The Litmus Test: Is Tourism in India All Set to Rise Again?

NOTE FOR READERS: This chapter was written in 2021–22, hence you may feel it is dated. The objective of its inclusion in the book is merely to convey the concept.

India cautiously decided to restart tourism, taking the first step towards bringing the tourism and hospitality industry back on its feet. How did it go?

After over six months of the worst period the Indian tourism industry had ever faced, it gradually yet cautiously bounced back. The Covid-19 pandemic had the country under lockdown since late March 2020, resulting in almost-complete travel restrictions, at least for the first couple of months. This partial and complete travel ban, coupled with the widespread pandemic havoc, has had a drastic impact on the tourism industry. The sector, for a brief period of time, was looking at a potential job loss of at least 38 million people directly or indirectly connected to the tourism industry.

Starting from October, the end-year period has always been a golden quarter for the tourism industry, owing to the long holidays of Dussehra, Diwali, Christmas, and all the way up to New Year. Families have always flocked to popular tourism destinations by the end of October, and the tourism season extends further up to early March, making October to March one of the most profitable sessions for the industry.

But due to the pandemic and a year-long hesitation to travel, the period proved to be a crucial test for the tourism industry. The industry had already seen a turn in events since October 2021 with the opening up of tourist places. But then, there was the hope that if the industry picked up pace, it could be the end of one of the worst periods. And if it had not, this could have meant that the industry could have slipped into an even more severe situation than anticipated earlier.

Is Everything Packed and Loaded for the Reopening?

Travel enthusiasts who have been cooped up for long inside their homes have some good news after quite a while. While popular travel destinations like Goa, Himachal Pradesh, and Karnataka had already started permitting travellers in small numbers, states like Uttar Pradesh have opened up almost all of their touristic destinations, including one of the most visited destinations of India, the Taj Mahal.

West Bengal, too, has reopened the forests in September. Darjeeling, one of the most famous hill stations in India, has also opened up for tourists.

One very important and aesthetic tourist destination for hill lovers—the valleys of Leh—is also accessible to tourists, but with proper precautions.

In addition to all these states, Tamil Nadu, Maharashtra, and even Andaman & Nicobar have opened up at least for some activities. But as the travel industry is seeing a gradual rise in bookings, the states might be planning something big for the upcoming quarter.

What Did October Bring?

Almost all of India will be ready to welcome tourists in the year-end quarter. And this had a steady start from October. The state of Odisha was overwhelmed with Golden Beach and Puri Beach receiving the prestigious eco-label 'Blue Flag' by the Foundation for Environmental Education (FEE). And this was followed by the opening up of the beaches of Gopalpur and Puri, along with the temples of Bhubaneswar and Konark. Sikkim, too, reopened to tourists and allowed homestays and hotels to start functioning at full capacity. Arunachal Pradesh resumed its tourism services citing how important the same was for the economy of the state.

However, none of the opening up of the states came without proper management and guidelines. Masks and physical distancing were mandatory for tourists. And in addition to this, people were expected to respect the sentiments of the locals as far as strictly following local rules were concerned.

October 2020 was a breath of fresh air for the tourism industry as well as for travel enthusiasts. It also provided a new lifeline to hotels in many tourist destinations. The question then was: How will things go post-October? Everything was quite uncertain. However, apart from all others, this test of October urges us to look into the biggest tourist hotspot during this season—Goa.

The Test of Goa

The tourist state of Goa has been getting itself ready for tourists for many months now. The clichéd destination is one of the most famous tourist getaways for foreign travellers in India. However, there is a slight misunderstanding regarding this. People think that foreign travel is Goa's only revenue generated from tourism. However, if Goa focused more on local Indian travellers, Goan tourism might garner even more revenue than from foreign travellers. Thus, despite an international ban on international flights, the last quarter of the year saw Goa's revenues bounce back due to the swarm of domestic travellers.

The long weekend at the start of October 2020 saw almost a half booking occupancy for starred hotels. This was a very promising figure for the entire tourism industry as it foreshadowed regular tourism if everything went well.

Now if the increased occupancy was a result of hotels reducing their rates by almost four times, we're not very sure. And frankly, it doesn't matter either. What matters is that slowly and steadily, people began to travel again. And all of that started in this quarter.

Similar to many other tourist destinations, the government of Goa had taken all the homestays under its control, making sure that the safety and hygiene standards of the places were up to the new mark. It also discouraged homestays that were offering accommodation for around 10 people in a single room, even if it was for a short period.

October proved to be a fairly balanced start for interested parties. States opened up their tourist destinations and integrated safety and hygienic protocols, resulting in an increased standard of cleanliness and precautions. And this proved to be a great step in boosting the economy of the states that depend primarily on tourism.

Hoteliers, Are Your Kitchens Ready to Deliver?

Food delivery, an already booming business line, has been accelerated even further due to customers' hesitation to go out to restaurants during the dark days of the pandemic. This provides an excellent opportunity for hotels that have been trying to make up for the prior period loss in their revenues. With the big leaguers like ITC, Taj Hotels, and Marriott already making the most of it, hoteliers should understand the whats, whys and hows of food delivery if they intend to stay relevant in the business.

Halting the tourism and hospitality industry completely for more than six months, the Covid-19 pandemic has caused a major shift in the way hotels do business. As tourism faced a ban, hotels that depended primarily on travellers for revenue had to look for more options. And this resulted in the emergence of several new business lines. While some hotels started providing exclusive laundry facilities to guests as well as customers, other hotels at exotic locations introduced a new work-from-hotel trend. Big hotel chains and groups provided live cooking sessions with their chefs. However, one thing that almost every hotel had to resort to was food delivery services.

From small regional hotels to big hotel chains like ITC, the Taj, and the Oberoi, every hotel has, in some way or the other, started delivering food to their customers. While some have collaborated with big food delivery services like Zomato and Swiggy, some that could afford their own delivery services have chosen to go that way. So if you're a hotelier yet to do this, here's why and how you should provide food delivery services to your customers.

Why Should Hotels Be Delivery-Ready?

Even before the pandemic, big players like Zomato and Swiggy enjoyed a huge demand for food delivery services. Swiggy ended 2018 with a whopping 1.5 million daily orders while Zomato followed closely behind with 1.2 million orders. And though there was a significant decrease in the number of orders during the lockdown, things have picked up really fast. Even after the lockdown restrictions have been lifted, some people are still hesitant to eat out. This poses a perfect opportunity for hotels to jump into the food delivery business. The shift in the eating patterns for people, away from dining out and towards ordering in, means that requirements for delivery services are on the rise, and it is time for hotels to consider this serious approach.

As far as the ease of process is concerned, it should not take much for hotels to jump into this new business line. If you have the resources ready, you can create your own application/ platform for ordering. Throw in a network of delivery providers, and voila, a new business line is ready for you! But in case you're short on resources, you could always partner with big providers that allow hotels to upload their menus and start delivering food without any hassle.

Giants like Swiggy and Zomato saw their highest-ever order peak for New Year's Eve 2020 despite the country being under a mild lockdown. And all this wouldn't have been possible without hotels providing their share of food for delivery. So, if you look at it, hotels, too, are helping the delivery providers and vice versa— *quid pro quo.*

Locals: How Big a Role Are They Going to Play?

One of the major factors that many hotels have constantly avoided is taking locals into account. Because most of their business comes from foreign travellers, hotels tend to avoid putting their resources towards locals. But seeing how food delivery outlets are more concerned about catering to the local radius, hotels need to transform this thinking.

Many hotels have introduced a compact menu of their signature dishes as a trial and are already seeing a positive response from residents in their vicinity. ITC hotels have partnered with Swiggy and are offering specially curated menus with local offerings for each region. They have also introduced a section on 'comfort food', indicating that ITC is not shying away from targeting local customers now. Marriott International, too, is attracting local customers, offering both takeaways and home delivery services.

Changing the Thinking: Marketing Experience versus Marketing Service

Apart from expanding their customer base, hotels should also change the way they approach their customers. Hotels tend to have high-falutin menus and descriptions that elevate the offerings to a premium level. They also offer customers an insight into how carefully and passionately the food has been prepared. And all of this is done to provide the dine-in guest with a complete experience of the hotel.

However, customers who order food online are in a completely different category from regular dine-in guests. They do not care about the experience as much as they care about the quality of the food, delivery time, and customer support. They're not going to be disappointed if the food isn't beautifully served. But they are going to be disappointed if their food is late. Thus, going forward with delivery services, hotels should avoid marketing the experience and instead market their delivery services.

What Resources Go into Making You Delivery-Ready?

Apart from preparing more food for delivery, providing a large kitchen for simultaneous operations, and packaging, hoteliers should aim for two major factors that can help them stand out in the business—marketing and analysis.

Marketing: If you're providing your own delivery services, earmark a sizable portion of your budget towards marketing. You will have to market the food as well as the services you're providing. Simply speaking, delivering online has its own benchmarks. You might be very good at hospitality, but if you do not meet the benchmarks, you're eventually going to suffer. So if you're providing your own delivery services, you need to invest resources into the speed and delivery times for your orders, including putting more resources into each—the products, the services, and the operations.

However, if you're partnering with a food delivery application/service provider, you can spare an individual to keep track of the operations while you invest more time and plan to provide a larger variety of food for your customers.

Analysis: Once you've decided to jump into the food delivery business, you'll have to keep a check on the ordering trends in your vicinity. Let the data be your guide. It can show you how your services are performing, including details for every dish ordered or searched for. Continuous learning through the data will give you an insight into what the locals crave and can help you choose which dishes to focus on. It also gives you the space to innovate and experiment safely with food choices without putting a dent in your revenue.

Creating another revenue stream for your business can be a challenging task if it is done without a vision. While the pandemic has made every hotelier scratch their heads to overcome this block, some visionaries have already taken the leap—after an intense amount of brainstorming, of course. From the looks of it, food delivery services from hotels are here to stay. It is therefore advisable for hotels to analyse the change, make the required calculations, and change their approach towards food delivery services.

Ian Schrager (Morgans Hotel Group) "People who are successful simply want it more than people who are not."

– Ian Schrager (Morgans Hotel Group)

Hotels and Events: What's it Going to be Like in a Post-Pandemic World?

The hospitality industry has taken quite a beating in the past few years due to the Covid-19 pandemic. Now that things have almost returned to normal, what will the new post-pandemic normal look like for hotels?

Covid-19 has stirred up a lot of trouble, changing both how our lives work and how we conduct business. Perhaps the most obviously affected industry in all this has been the hospitality industry, and that's not just from a travel and reservation point of view. MICE travel and events—the large source of revenue of the industry—were impacted greatly. But it did not stop there; the ripple effects spread to non-business events, too.

Take weddings as an example. An over ₹100k-crore industry, the market for wedding events in India is huge, to say the least. But during the Covid years, there were concerns about such large gatherings. And with government restrictions on the number of people who could attend such events, the big, vibrant Indian affairs reduced considerably.

The global crisis also led to mass cancellations of travel and events and a shift towards a more virtual model. And since events were a major source of revenue for the hospitality industry, the industry was hit hard.

When the world opened up again, the hotel industry had to prepare for an even greater shift post-pandemic, which brought in its wake complications that would effectively change how the industry worked for the foreseeable future.

Hotels and Events: During the Pandemic

The pandemic came as a major blow to the operations of the hospitality industry. As restrictions were placed on travel and large gatherings, important revenue sources for hotels disappeared. Concerts were cancelled, business gatherings paused, and celebrations limited to a select number of people. Most events were held virtually, or hotels had to limit the number of guests to prevent the spread of the novel coronavirus.

Of course, the event industry as a whole suffered, with mass cancellations and postponements of pre-scheduled events like concerts, marriages, and more. This indirectly affected a huge part of the hospitality industry—the one that was dependent on booking rooms and function halls, restaurants, spas, and other commercial spaces as a major source of revenue. And since all this came to a halt during Covid, business was badly hit.

Hotels and Events: Post-Pandemic

When businesses and public spaces opened ed up, the hospitality industry, too, tried to get back on its feet in the following months. However, it was not an easy road for hotel owners. For one, even as lockdowns were lifted across the globe, the psychological fear in public perception lingered for a longer period of time. The paranoia about health and hygiene that had implanted itself into the forefront of our brains did not disappear soon, considering that the virus kept appearing in different strains in some part of the globe or the other.

So, how did the hospitality industry ensure its survival and effectively recover business? To answer that question, we need to look at several key elements and issues that cropped up in the coming months.

- **Hosting and accommodating large crowds**

Perhaps the biggest challenge the industry faced was the issue of how to manage and accommodate crowds when hosting events. Big Indian weddings, for example, drive huge crowds of thousands of people to hotel gardens and halls.

However, the pandemic had necessitated obvious government restrictions on such large gatherings. A hall that could previously easily fit 500 to 1,000 guests could now seat only 200 guests to follow social distancing norms strictly.

The same was true for corporate conferences or small events. While the number of guests may have been small, the space required to accommodate, with social distancing protocols in mind, would be at least three to four times more. To counter this, hotels had to open more spaces to improve their infrastructure to the extent possible.

- **Resuming travel for events**

Once the lockdown was over, both domestic and international travel resumed slowly, yet steadily. It took a while for things to get back to normal, but there was no doubt that travel had become an indispensable part of our lives—business and corporate (leisure travel bounced back too, but a bit later). A glimmer of uncertainty lay in how much of a norm virtual events would become by the time borders were relaxed again and travel could resume safely.

During the ongoing pandemic, it became apparent that a lot of the things that previously required our physical presence could just as easily (if not more) be done behind the screen. While leisure travel was likely to resume pretty quickly, the same perhaps could not be said for concerts as they involved crowds of thousands and saw success in holding—and even earning revenue—from virtual events during the pandemic.

- **Implementing safety and hygiene measures**

An important deciding factor in how soon hotels were able to return to normal functioning was the health and hygiene measures they put in place to ensure guest safety. It fell to them to ensure that health regulations were being met, and they had to bear some measure of accountability in that regard.

Even if the hotel was able to put such measures in place, they would have to find ways to assure both event planners and attendees that all precautions were being taken and that attending the event would not put their health at risk—a task that wasn't easy in the climate of those days.

- **Investing costs and resources into recovery**

One thing that you may have come to realise while reading the points I have covered above is that, before anything else, hotels were going to need ample reserves of capital and resources. The pandemic saw an almost total reduction of revenue for hotels, yet, resuming regular operations itself was going to take time and money—both of which the hotels were undoubtedly short of.

Besides the costs that were to go into marketing efforts to build back their guest lists once again and assure them of the safety of staying with them, hotels also needed to invest heavily in updating their technology and infrastructure. Guests were likely to prefer minimum contact during their stay, which would necessitate the presence of services such as express check-outs from their hotel rooms, mobile keys, sanitisation booths, and more.

The more reassured the guests felt, the easier it would be for the hotel to get back into the swing of things. However, providing this assurance was going to take significant capital investment on their part—something that was not easy in that financial climate.

The future of events and hospitality was rife with uncertainty. Still, this was not the first time the industry was faced with such a challenge. Despite all the risks, it's undeniable that travel has become integral to human well-being and life. It is unlikely that we are going to give up on it anytime soon. The likes of Covid-19 and its consequences had never been seen before. But with proper planning and measures in place, the hospitality industry was able to get through this period, too, like it has done many times before.

"The great advantage of a hotel is that
it is a refuge from home life"

– George Bernard Shaw

Post Covid-19 Hotel Architecture Challenges: Restoring Consumer Confidence

Of all the sectors affected by the pandemic, the hotel industry has probably been the hardest hit. But hoteliers are pouring all their energy into getting back on their feet. Part of their strategy deals with changing hotel architecture so that their establishments are safe for their guests and in compliance with the local rules on health and hygiene.

Did you know that China's bubonic outbreak in 1855 forever changed the design of everything from door thresholds to drainpipes and building foundations? Or that the introduction of sewage systems in 19th-century England was prompted by the many epidemics that ravaged the land and its people. These sewage systems required the roads above them to be wider and straighter, thus influencing the modern street grid. Also, the 'wipe clean' aesthetic of modernism with light-flooded structures was in part a result of tuberculosis, inspiring an era of white rooms, tiled bathrooms, and the ever-present mid-century recliner chair.

Form has always followed the fear of infection, just as much as function. From wide streets lined with trees to antibacterial brass doorknobs, architecture has, in part, always been shaped by disease.

With the Covid-19 pandemic leaving each of us in socially distanced isolation with offices abandoned, shops shuttered, and cities reduced to ghost towns, it's hard not to wonder about the lasting effects it might have on architecture as a whole. And while that would make for a very interesting discourse, here, we will be focusing only on the impact that Covid-19 is likely to have on hotel architecture.

The industry knew very well that even after the dust settled on this pandemic and we ventured out to find what people are calling the 'new normal' for the hospitality industry, it would not be 'business as usual'. People would hesitate to step inside hotels and restaurants. Therefore, to recuperate from the financial losses, it would take months or even years. Certain hospitality veterans who have seen their fair share of tumult believed that eventually there would be a complete return to normal.

Till then, however, the industry had to make some changes—big and small—to help it along.

Hotel Architecture Going Forward

One hotel in Hong Kong has already switched its entire renovation plan in anticipation of changing guest behaviour. The property was closed for renovation in February 2020, and within two months, the management realised that the renderings drawn before the pandemic might be off the mark when the hotel reopens.

So today, they are considering additional investments, such as negative pressure floors that prevent cross-contamination from room to room, built-in thermal scanners, a mobile check-in system, and no-touch elevator control panels.

On the redesign front, they implemented greater spatial layouts not only in public areas but also in their restaurants and club lounges to give their guests more space and privacy. Their restaurant has separate sections that complement each other, two private dining areas, and an alfresco area apart from the main dining section.

Their conference rooms and function areas also make space for private parties and small meetings. What's more, they have also upgraded the space with IT capabilities, given the rising trend for video conferences.

The use of materials and fabrics changed, too. The hotel asked its project consultants to look into easily cleanable materials that are resistant to bacterial infection, including tabletops, flooring, and seating. For a more hygienic dining experience, their buffets now provide single portions and sneeze guards.

The Hong Kong hotel is not the only one making drastic changes right now. A chain of hotels in Bangkok has also changed the design of its guest rooms that now feature hard-surface floors accented by area rugs instead of fully carpeted floors. They did this because area rugs are easier to disinfect and clean. Upon further revision, they did away with other unnecessary clutter like bed runners, decorative pillows, etc.

The hotel has reconfigured all public areas, including the lobby, executive lounges, restaurants, and pool terraces in a way that allows groups to separate from each other. Furthermore, they have reduced the maximum capacities in elevators and marked the floors with safe-distance indicators where queues may form.

Apart from carrying out these stringent health and safety practices, tech will likely be everywhere in the hospitality industry. With the astonishing cuts in costs to incremental revenue-generating areas zero-maintenance buildings, touch-free interactions, and technology-based sanitisation will gradually become commonplace in hotels around the world.

Architecture that's Aligned with the Environment

The design of hotels will also become more environmentally conscious. With the positive environmental changes already occurring in the post-pandemic design concept, designers are motivated now, more than ever, to weave environmentally conscientious design choices into the spaces that they design for guests and staff.

And for those confined in big cities, Danu Kennedy, design director for Parts and Labor, predicts a greater return to nature, sunlight, and fresh air. She says, "Hospitality may need to pivot towards a more exterior rather than interior offering". Parts and Labor Design is one of New York's leading architectural/design agencies specializing in hospitality projects.

The focus on emotional well-being, self-care, and wellness will also become more prevalent. "Architects and designers will need to look at how to make our new 'defensive' spaces (think plexi'd off check-in desks) come off as warm and embracing. The challenge will lie in balancing the need to mitigate worry while at the same time providing spaces that invite guests to relax and enjoy themselves. Designers will need to tap into the psychology and emotional wellbeing of the guests more so than before," says W. Brian Smith, co-founder of Studio Tack, a design and developmental group based in Brooklyn.

Guests will also be looking more closely at what they get in-room, rather than property-wide. So now, and moving forward, hotels will have to develop new plans that bring on-site amenities into the guests' rooms as they may be averse to unnecessary interactions for the time being. Wellness facilities will likely become a fundamental part of what the guests look for when booking a hotel.

The executive director of a renowned hospitality company agrees that privacy will become even more private, thus increasing the demand for in-room well-being practices. Their company has created what it calls a 'White Room' in response to this, which is a clean and sleek space designed to cut out distractions so that guests can reboot through guided meditation.

As you may be well aware, the hospitality industry has far-reaching effects on other sectors of industry. For instance, it enjoys a symbiotic relationship with the travel industry. As accommodation is so easily accessible, people have fewer qualms about travelling for holidays, education, pilgrimage, or business.

Hence, it generates business for travel agents, airlines, cruises, car rentals, tour guides, and souvenir dealers, among others. Within the hotels themselves, it then generates demand not only for accommodation but also for food and beverages, meeting spaces, business centres, spas, banquet and exhibition halls, commercial spaces, etc. Therefore, it is imperative that it gets up and running again soon.

While the future did look bleak during the pandemic, right now, I, too, share the optimistic view that the business has bounced back to normal, if not a slightly improved version of it. Humans are resilient and innately social creatures; therefore, we will always gather to eat, drink, travel, and make merry.

The Re-Rise of Tourism: How to Bolster Confidence in the New Breed of Nervous Travellers

The travel and hospitality industry was the hardest hit by the Covid pandemic. But it picked itself up once countries relaxed their travel guidelines. Hotels have opened their doors again. That said, hotels and tour operators will have to remember that they're now dealing with a new brand of travellers, one that's increasingly nervous and extremely suspicious.

As much as the travel industry suffered due to the travel restrictions placed in the wake of the Covid-19 pandemic outbreak, it has bounced back now. With people claiming the period between October-February, 2020 as the 'litmus test' for the industry, it is yet to be seen if the damage received will be compensated quickly in some destinations or if this is just a step in a long journey of bouncing back. Whatever be the case, the travel industry needs to address one very important issue immediately—the psychological hesitation of nervous travellers.

People who were cooped up inside their homes are looking to travel, some after a long period. But they are faced with a dilemma. On the one hand, their willingness to travel is pushing them to start their journeys, while on the other hand, their scepticism with regard to the dangers of various variants of Covid-19 is still holding them back. This hesitation exists not just with regard to the places they're planning to visit but also in their modes of travel. A little less than half of the people adamantly stated that they were in no mood to fly to their travel destination. This hesitation was not just against airlines but against all public modes of transport, publicly accessible places, and homestays and B&Bs.

As the tourism industry was eager to rope in these nervous travel enthusiasts, they took steps to provide them with enough assurance and credibility, thereby assuring them and eliminating all hesitation. This helped the travel industry in bolstering their revenue and attracting more travellers through word of mouth.

Personally, I believe that the industry must categorize different travellers according to the hesitations they have. Only then can they understand how to win back their trust. Let's take a look at the type of travellers and the solutions that the tourism industry can provide to them.

Bleisure: The Business Traveller

One of the most revenue-generating travel modes for the industry, business travel, was partially or completely halted due to the Covid-19 outbreak. Many managers and employees had their reservations regarding travelling for the sake of work, even if there was complete assurance from the company's end, implying that they were doubtful about not just the accommodation or amenities but also the hygiene and safety measures.

India was ranked second under bleisure travelling (business plus leisure), with more than 72% of Indian travellers extending their business trips according to a report by booking.com. Companies developed contingency plans to avoid travel, instead opting for telecommunication and video conferences

From the company's end regarding employee travel plans, clear and precise rules of business travel were initiated, which were understood by all. People were briefed on what was covered during the trip and what was not. In addition, there were clear instructions and policies on what people should do if they did not feel safe during the trip.

As far as hotels were concerned, they made sure that the travellers were informed of all the safety measures that were put in place in the hotel. Guests were provided with a clear list of protocols to be followed in the hotel. Practically all hotels had go-to persons readily available if a business traveller needed any kind of help.

The No-Fly Traveller

As was evident from surveys conducted by top travel agencies, many travellers were hesitant in choosing flying as their means of travel. Almost 40% of the people who planned to travel were sure that they would prefer to fly with their national or domestic carrier rather than choosing an international one.

Airlines, too, were impacted hugely due to the Covid-19 outbreak. Travel restrictions, coupled with travel hesitation, resulted in a tremendous loss of revenue. Initially, when travel began again, people were shying away from flying. That did not augur well for airlines the world over.

To counter this travel hesitation and to attract travellers again, the airlines decided to offer reductions in fares. While this was not a very smart strategy for small airlines, which had no or little reserves, it was considered the most foolproof method to get travel by air back on track again.

This brings us to another side of the story. When people were hesitant about air travel, they were not likely to travel long distances by air. This factor triggered yet another marketing strategy—to operate additional flights to domestic destinations, metros, and mini metros, spreading the safe destinations by word of mouth, and keeping the business afloat.

The Local Traveller

As is evident from the points I've made above, people were hesitant to travel long distances, especially when they were not in control of their modes of travel. If asked for a preference, there was a good chance that people would have preferred local destinations over foreign ones. While this was a blow to foreign travel, local governments used this as the perfect opportunity to focus more on local destinations. For example, people in India were more likely to travel to local destinations like Manali, Srinagar, or Kerala (and they were encouraged, too). This helped them to get over their hesitation to travel and made them comfortable with the idea of travelling in the post-Covid period. Companies also provided safe sanitising solutions (like sanitised parking services) and local modes of transport.

As far as stays were concerned, local stays were less favoured than big hotel chains, since the latter were more trusted. They created awareness, through their social media handles and marketing mailers, that they were ready for business. Their security protocols, hygiene protocols, and credibility were clearly visible, attracting more and more people.

Health Care-First Travellers

People were aware that travel during those times came with certain risks. And therefore, they preferred to go to destinations that had proper health care facilities. In the initial days, there was no vaccine in sight, and people relied solely on prevention and precautions.

Hotels made their customers feel safer by tying up with local health care facilities for routine check-ups and tests. They could get individual travellers tested constantly, if such a need arose. They also suggested sightseeing spots that had taken strict precautions against the pandemic. Most of these hotels ensured that these measures were given due publicity in the local print media for the information of travellers.

Credibility-First Travellers

Many hesitant travellers trusted only big brands for their travel. They needed the assurance of a brand that would ensure their well-being during the trip. Towards this end, most branded chain hotels and large airlines made sure that they publicised their safety protocols—PPE-wearing individuals, constant sanitisation, and contactless services. To further their effort in customer confidence building, these hotels and airlines also requested organisations like the Centers for Disease Control (CDC), the World Health Organization (WHO), and local governments to consider a certification program for those who were in compliance with their health and safety protocols.

Communication also played a very important role here as people were relying on the information they received from the hotels or airlines about their safety standards. Hotels targeted their frequent customers and stayed in constant contact with them through emails and calls, providing them with continuous updates on their safety measures.

As the tourism and hospitality industry rises again to accommodate travel enthusiasts, it is faced with many challenges. From keeping safety standards at an impeccable best to motivating nervous travellers to overcome their hesitation, the list is quite long. However, keeping in mind the fact that people have been cooped up inside their homes for so long and that governments and the travel industry have adopted some of the best hygiene standards, the task feels doable. The road to the 're-rise' of travelling was tough. Looking back, I can only say, it was a difficult period but provided good learnings for the industry!

"Courteous treatment will make a customer
a walking advertisement"

– James Cash Penney

How Technology Made the Hotel Experience Safer in the Post-Covid-19 World

Three months after the pandemic hit the country, life stood still, and nothing seemed right. We witnessed death, infections, a crumpled economy, and restricted movements due to strict lockdowns. However, we also looked forward to a time when restrictions would be lifted and life would get better.

Years from now, when we look back at this phase, we'll be sipping our tea with gratitude for the brave souls who helped us to overcome this and a spoonful of appreciation for the opportunity to rebuild our lives.

Along with chaos and loss of life, business, too, has had its fair share of difficulties with small and large industries facing the consequences of this pandemic. Many start-ups have closed shop, laying off employees at an unprecedented rate. Among the bigger sectors, hospitality and tourism have probably faced the worst of it. With the whole country in lockdown, there was minimal travel domestically and zero travel internationally, which brought the travel industry to a grinding halt. As peer *ETHospitalityWorld*, the Indian hospitality industry (standalone hotel segments and hotel chains only) lost around ₹960–1,100 crores. This is alarming because it took into account only 5% of accommodations, excluding alternate accommodation sectors like B&Bs, homestays, and guest houses.

To be frank we were quite unsure about how we would tackle the issue of getting back on track. It needed innovative strategies, hard decisions, and serious efforts.

I don't mean to imply that the travel and hospitality industry could never recover from a loss of such stature. But it required more than just immense effort or planning; it also needed understanding and trust-building to get the industries through this.

Trust-building was of critical importance. Our industry, by its very nature, involves a fair amount of human contact. Covid-19 made us suspicious of each other because it was hard to say who was a carrier of the virus and how it was spread. Even when the government-imposed lockdown was lifted and Covid-19 cases tapered down substantially, people were still hesitant. That's why everything that we did after Covid-19 had to focus on building one very important thing—trust.

Recently, we've seen that people, irrespective of age or generation, have become very receptive towards technology. The widespread usage of India's Covid-19 tracker app, Arogya Setu, has proved this claim substantially. It has also proved that if technology is integrated into various industries, it'll result in a strengthening of bonds between service providers and customers. In view of that, let us see what a must for the hospitality industry is after Covid-19.

Hotels in Life after Covid-19

Life after Covid-19 will be different from what it was before in a lot of different ways. More reliance on technology will be a great trust-building tool, as will tracking, monitoring, and sanitising.

Transparency: One of the biggest factors in trust-building is transparency. Customers arriving at hotels need to be sure that the hotel is safe for them and their families. They need to know about all the services, sanitation, occupancy, or equipment of the hotels. A simple application that updates people on how their laundries are done, the cleaning standard of the rooms they occupy, the safety of the food they're eating, and details on their washrooms' sanitisation should do the trick. Consider making your identity around cleanliness. If you're clean, be visible.

Maximum effort: Big hotel chains have always prioritised their cleanliness and hygiene. But they'll have to put in even more effort to maintain impeccable standards of hygiene. Hotels can promote the use of UV lights, as these detect even the slightest dirt. Sanitisers have to be made more readily available than before, preferably among high-touch, unavoidable areas like elevators, unless they are foot-operated. Wipes and towels should also be available (with proper packaging) for customers in case they want to wipe down areas or corners of their rooms to their satisfaction.

Constant updates: The battle against Covid-19 was long and tiring. Constant monitoring, tracking, and validation of all the guests was necessary. People were informed that their co-travellers and co-dwellers were safe to be with. Moreover, if anyone was found Covid-19 positive, they were sent for treatment with proper care, and the other guests were informed accordingly.

Long-term planning: Hotels should also aim at targeting millennials, preferably by offering big discount coupons or add-ons. Technologically, millennials are very well-informed. Though there is no trust barrier between technology and people from any generation now, millennials are more likely to understand these as they were born into the technological age. This would then shift the focus of millennials from B&Bs and homestays, benefiting hotels in the long term.

With overall priorities sorted out, hotels must also look at the specific areas they can target and flourish in, generating revenue even in times like that. First, we examined what they were achieving then and how much they would achieve post Covid-19.

What Hotels Are Doing Right Now

Most hotels were closed for business during the lockdown, and even after that, for a substantial period. Some hotels that were open had offered their space for use by local governments for travellers during the emergency or converted them into quarantine facilities with enhanced Covid protocols. Hotels all over the world started vigorously practising the hygiene policies of hospitals and wellness centres. With mandatory mobile check-ins/check-outs instead of the usual front desk services and long lines, cashless payments, online menus, online orders, and no concierge access to rooms, hotels tried to implement contactless service to the extent feasible.

All hotels that were partially operational implemented policies in line with the government's guidelines. Some of the big hotel chains in India updated their detailed list of protocols, available for public view. Some partnered with the world's leading testing, inspection, and certification agencies to validate their protocols and efforts. From details about front desk services to back offices, all the information was readily available on their websites. This appreciation-worthy practice was a very useful trust-building exercise during the pandemic.

Public areas like restrooms, elevators, lobbies, etc., were constantly cleaned with hospital-grade disinfectants and procedures. The dining experience, if operated, was thoughtfully curated keeping in mind limited gatherings in restaurant areas for safety.

Apart from all these services, big hotel chains also collaborated with online portals like Zomato and Swiggy for home delivery of food. It was a way to generate additional revenue, and more importantly, to build trust with their customers and retain their skilled kitchen staff, which eventually helped in the long run.

The policies that were followed, including transparency and the use of technology to minimise contact, were definitely applause-worthy.

What Hotels Should Aim For

To win back the trust of people, and to make them feel safe about accepting hotels again, hotels initiated certain tactical actions that enhanced the guest's experience to a completely new and safe level. They knew that guests were not going to accept anything less.

Hence, in order to reinforce trust, hotels opted for a completely contactless, technology-driven experience. However, since the hospitality industry is people-centric, with guests expecting personal contact, it proved to be quite a challenge initially.

Although it may sound far-fetched, some hotels in the US have already been trying an AI relay room service. As soon as the order is placed, hotel staff load items into a relay, which then navigates around the property using Wi-Fi, on-board cameras, and sensors. Guests can then retrieve items from within the robot's storage compartment when it reaches their door, thus minimising contact.

Big hotels have also been trying this in the luggage section. From a practical perspective, someone would still have to open car doors and remove luggage from the vehicle. But a robot could then take over—swiftly transporting luggage to the guest room.

Embracing technology and integrating it into our work culture definitely built trust with the guests. Replacing the front desk human contact with an automated service is surely going to help people trust the hygiene and safety protocols of the hotel. However, it has its limitations. It will undoubtedly be missing the warmth of a smile upon arriving at the hotel. Similarly, a robotic concierge will never be able to match human empathy and warmth. Nevertheless, it definitely lessens the risk of contamination, which was the most essential factor then.

We had to compromise our longing for a warm, familiar, and courteous smile for some time. However, I am positive that hotels have emerged as a sophisticated, empathetic, secure, and cautious industry, completely transformed by technology. Thus, as was the demand of the time, hotels embraced technology to offer guests a safe and exciting experience.

Six Reasons Why the Hotel Industry Will Bounce Back from the Pandemic

When the COVID-19 pandemic hit, it left no corner of our lives untouched. The world has never seen a biological crisis on this large a scale before. Businesses all across the globe were forced to shut down due to the lack of operations, revenue, and support, and the hospitality industry was hit the hardest. Travel restrictions all over the world led to cancellations and empty hotels, with no telling how and when the situation may stabilise enough that things may return to normal.

The challenges in this particular scenario seemed insurmountable. But even back then, I was confident that the industry would recover from these hard times, just as it had pulled through other downturns in the past. No doubt, it was going to take time—a lot of time—but we were going to pull through. And I had six good reasons to give me hope.

The Travel Bug, Intensified

During the lockdown, and even in the following months that placed restrictions on movements domestically and internationally, I noticed a build-up of restlessness and an increasing desire to step out of our homes. People were restless to reclaim their spirit of exploration and once the situation became safer and the rules were relaxed, there were going to be many who would be itching to leave their confining environments behind for a much-needed break. In fact, there was going to be a rise in demand for experiential packages and stays, such as spas and retreats, as people tried to move on from the pandemic and enjoy the luxuries of life once again.

International travel, on the other hand, would probably stay on the low for a few months after the borders opened up due to public apprehension and financial barriers. However, we could expect local travel and short getaways to become more popular during the initial recovery days as people took advantage of the freedom they had regained.

Learning from the Past

COVID-19 isn't the first time a global crisis has led to empty halls and pockets. Many hoteliers have lived through past financial crises, and those of us who haven't would've certainly heard about them. While it may have been a bit too optimistic to say that hoteliers were ready to face this challenge head-on, their past experience had equipped them with the skills and mental acumen to deal with it.

No doubt, it would take them longer to plan a strategy that could be implemented with success to overcome the issues specific to the pandemic. But they did have some insight into *what not to do* during an emergency like this. Enough regulations and advisories were being issued by government bodies, medical professionals, and industry experts to guide their decisions, make strong plans of action, and avoid knee-jerk reactions like the kind of rate slashing that occurred due to the 2007 financial crisis.

Technology is the Way Forward

Even as the industry was facing a significant financial setback, hoteliers had access to more resources and technologies than ever before to implement creative solutions and recover their losses.

One key factor that would have had a major hand in any hotel's recovery was how they responded to customer fears. There was a lot of apprehension in the air, with customers worrying about not picking up the virus. It was important that guest experiences at hotels helped to reassure them. Innovations like mobile keys would go a long way in alleviating guest concerns and reducing contact between individuals, which was particularly important in a post-social distancing environment. Those hoteliers that were early adopters of such technologies would have benefitted the most and they would've been particularly well-equipped to weather the storm.

The Importance of Engagement

It also became apparent that hotels that were actively engaging with their customers through digital media had an edge. After all, there was no use in having all these technologies at your disposal without using them to communicate with your audience.

It was gratifying to see that many hotels had started productively using this time to create better relationships with customers as well as tailoring their marketing and promotional strategies according to the situation. They were more in tune with customer needs, and thus, knew exactly how to communicate with their audience to fulfil their business goals. They were quick to plan, adapt, and implement marketing strategies, which definitely paid off once the restrictions were lifted.

We were a long way off from the days when all marketing stood for was selling rooms. Post-pandemic, hoteliers became aware that selling experiences and building connections were more important than pushing out marketing content. That is why hotels that prioritised customers even during the pandemic fared well when the world opened up.

A Shift in the Market

A major issue that the industry faced once things returned to normal was people's reluctance to travel to those areas that were hit the hardest during the pandemic. Big hotel chains were able to wait this out by focusing on other market segments that were not hit as badly by the virus, which is where travel for leisure shifted to until the scars from the pandemic healed. Meanwhile, small boutique hotels and homestays might become more popular due to people favouring stays with less of a crowd.

There was also a possibility that travellers would prefer the predictability and safety of traditional hotels once travel resumed, mainly because they could guarantee guests a clean, dependable, and safe stay. This would help hotels regain those customers who, in recent years, had started preferring services like Airbnb over traditional hotel stays.

One Last Note of Hope

Perhaps the biggest source of hope for despondent hoteliers came from China, which was already showing signs of recovery after dealing with its own crisis. Slowly but steadily, Chinese businesses started returning to normal in the second half of 2021.

And when China's capital, Beijing, relaxed quarantine rules, it led to a surge in searches and bookings for air travel and hotels. In fact, within just a few months, the occupancy rate almost tripled, revealing an eagerness among people to step out and travel again. This definitely sent out a positive message to the rest of the world and gave everyone hope of returning to business as usual in a few years.

The one thing we must remember is that we're all in the same boat after this pandemic. Many resorts and hotels have had to rebuild and even start from scratch. Hope comes from the undeniable fact that travel and tourism are deeply ingrained in our lives; and we will all return to it once things become normal and we put this crisis behind us. Yes, it was slow going for a while, but I had no doubt that the industry would soon be back on its feet, with more experiences to learn from and better prepared for the future.

"Success seems to be connected to action.
Successful people keep moving.
They make mistakes, but they don't quit."

– Conrad Hilton

Social Distancing and Its Impact

In the age of coronavirus, most of us were either stuck at home or working on the frontlines. We were all telling each other to take precautions and practise social distancing. But I often used to wonder whether the term 'social distancing' is even correct.

During the pandemic, there was one universal message going around in the world—that everyone needed to stay home and avoid physical contact with other people at all costs. We called it social distancing, and you could see everyone, from major news channels to your next-door neighbour, using this term free in their day-to-day language. There was absolutely no one on this planet who was unaware of this term.

However, was this really the term we should have been using? In times of a global pandemic, were we really supposed to 'socially' distance ourselves? With the spread of Covid-19 showing no signs of slowing down, it was more important than ever for us to get in touch with our social lives and stay connected with people around us so we didn't end up feeling isolated. In such times, the phrase social distancing could be misleading.

Why do I say that? Because the word 'social' itself has come to be associated with something entirely different of late.

At one point in time, the word 'social' meant going out with friends, meeting new people, or generally being outside and enjoying our lives. While that's true to some degree even now, it's undeniable that there's been a huge cultural reset in the past couple of years.

Take the word 'social' itself. Hasn't it become natural to immediately complete the term with 'media' as soon as you hear it? Being social has become synonymous with social media. Updating your Instagram story to keep your followers in the loop in your life, tweeting out little titbits from your day on X, and interacting with millions of people online... it's become a natural extension of our lives. And these days, to limit the definition of 'social' to just those old-fashioned get-togethers, dinner dates, or parties would be remiss of us, don't you think?

It was then that I decided to propose an alternative to the term 'social distancing': physical distancing.

Governments and organisations all around the world were urging their citizens to stay at home with their close friends or family and avoid large crowds or social events that could lead to further spread of the virus. While I agreed with this approach, I believe that the term 'physical distancing' is more suited to the occasion.

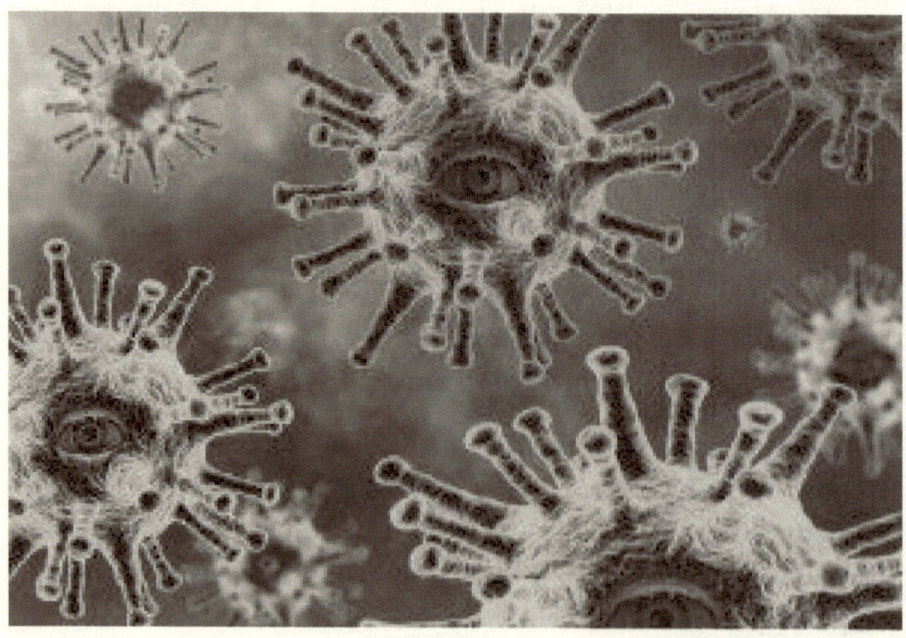

Think about it. Isn't that what we're essentially doing? Creating a physical distance between each other for the sake of our (and their) safety and well-being. Besides, the term 'physical distancing' immediately conveyed what we were supposed to do, leaving absolutely no room for misunderstanding. You tell someone to physically distance themselves from you, and they'll keep themselves at a distance from you. Ask people to socially distance themselves from you, and you might not get invited to their son's marriage!

Jokes aside, there's yet another reason why it was important to be mindful of the terms we used back then. While physical distancing was essential to keep us safe from the novel coronavirus, we needed 'social proximity' to keep us sane amidst this lockdown.

What We Absolutely Should Not Do: Social Distancing

Humans are social beings. Even those who say they don't like to be as socially active as the average extrovert would admit that they would eventually go insane without some form of social contact. And especially during times when our anxiety levels were running high, a gentle hug, a hand to hold, or a heart-to-heart talk with a loved one are often our best sources of comfort. But alas! Physical distancing makes that impossible.

However, instead of completely isolating ourselves from the outside world and going crazy inside our homes, we needed to find different ways to stay connected with each other. Without some form of camaraderie and a feeling of being connected, a sense of loneliness could creep into our subconscious mind, which could take a toll on our well-being.

It was definitely not good to isolate ourselves. In fact, it was the time to use the tools we had at our disposal and find newer ways to interact and connect with each other... you know, be social with each other.

Being 'Social' in the Midst of a Pandemic

The global slowdown and the months that followed were tough on everyone, but we also saw the world coming together like never before. At the forefront of this was social media. Whether was through using apps like Zoom and Houseparty for video calls or finding unique ways to keep ourselves entertained at home, social media made a variety of social interactions possible.

Artists were holding live concerts from their homes, and virtual events were cropping up everywhere. Many of us were revisiting old hobbies or using this time to learn new things online. And it wasn't just entertainment. We were also using social media to power a social movement in the midst of all this. Young people were volunteering to deliver groceries for older people who were living alone, funds were being set up to aid relief causes for the less fortunate, and all over, we were hearing inspiring stories about individuals doing their bit to get through this pandemic together.

These kinds of social interactions did more than just uplift our spirits. They expanded the boundaries of our four walls and helped us to virtually escape the confines of our homes and travel the world. Instead of feeling lonely, useless, or depressed, we were able to find new ways to add meaning to our lives, and that of others. Furthermore, it gave families so many different ways to bond with each other, even if they were kept apart by physical distance. And we really have social media to thank for all this.

Now, I am sure you're going to think of all this niggling over phrases as a whim. But I'm old-fashioned, and I believe that words are important and the messaging behind them should be clear. I admit that social distancing probably borrows from the word 'social' as we used to understand it before, which stood for socialising and mingling with people. But given that the word has grown to mean so much more in the 21st century, we should reconsider its use as well, shouldn't we? Especially when the phrase 'physical distancing' is abundantly clear in what it wants to convey.

Having said that, I am well aware that habits once formed are difficult to change, especially after social distancing as a phrase caught on. So I decided to make a compromise. I told everyone around me to embrace the spirit of social proximity while following the rules of physical distancing. Now that we had the tools and the good fortune of being able to stay connected and bring comfort to each other, albeit virtually, it was time to create stronger bonds and get through these tough times as a community. It was time to reach out to loved ones, people you had lost touch with, and even strangers on the internet who needed a gentle ear. And of course, it was important to wash your hands and practise physical distancing at all times!

"I tell our people all the time 'Success is never final',
and it isn't, it's a lot easier sometimes to get
to the top than it is to stay there."

– J. Willard Marriott

How The Hospitality Industry Prepared for Life After Covid-19!

'Unprecedented'—that was the word people were using to describe the pandemic that had brought the world to its knees. And how! All the tried and tested measures of crisis management seemed ineffective. Industry veterans had to mull over some out-of-the-box measures to keep the tourism and hospitality industry afloat; they had to find different ways to use the time they had those days.

I think we would all agree that life during Covid-19 was difficult for everyone. No one could have predicted that in a matter of just a few weeks, the world would come to a grinding halt. In an effort to isolate, control, and stop the spread of the disease, travel bans were put in place, businesses were forced to close down, people were told not to leave their homes, and once-bustling cities were utterly devoid of life.

As the devastating pandemic engulfed the whole world, many major industries prepared themselves for huge setbacks. However, with domestic and international travel restricted, the tourism and hospitality industries around the world took the worst hit. India was in a state of complete lockdown from March 2020 to May 2020 and this had a direct impact on the travel and hospitality sectors. While the complete lockdown was removed in May 2020, travel restrictions continued with very strict pandemic protocols. The halting of all transportation systems resulted in one of the worst revenue dips that the travel industry had seen in years.

The hospitality industry was not doing any better, with many corporate gatherings, MICE (meetings, incentives, conferences and exhibitions), leisure meetings, and events postponed or cancelled. As the industry was entirely dependent on travel, trade, and tourism, the massive spate of cancellations eroded the ability of hotels across India to keep their doors open, resulting in worrisome losses.

Whether it was a small vendor or a big-time tours and travel giant, the cascading effects of Covid-19 on the tourism and hospitality industries was unnerving, to say the least. However, regardless of how tough things got, I knew in my heart that the industry was capable of overcoming these obstacles.

How Covid-19 affected Tourism and Hospitality Worldwide

If we were to go by sheer numbers, tourism sectors around the world were in a state of constant crisis since the outbreak of the virus, as reported by the World Travel and Tourism Council (WTTC). Almost 50 million jobs (including 30 million in Asia itself) were lost worldwide. This meant that the travel industry had shrunk by about 25% in 2020 alone. The crunch in the hospitality sector had put around four million jobs at stake worldwide. And the first to see massive layoffs within this industry were the casual and contractual staff.

The Impact of Covid-19 in India

Prime tourist attractions like Rajasthan and Kerala, which were otherwise immensely popular during the summers, witnessed empty rooms in the summer of 2020. Even before India was locked down, the fear of the coronavirus had resulted in a huge drop in airfares.

The Indian hospitality industry experienced a humongous loss of around ₹620 cr. The worst blow was felt by alternate accommodations (hostels, homestays, bed-and-breakfasts, etc.), which made up a good percentage of the industry.

While the industry crunch affected many travel giants like MakeMyTrip and TripAdvisor, smaller businesses and start-ups were left with no choice but to either close shop or resort to staff or salary cuts.

Steps Taken for the Recovery of the Travel Industry

Amidst this crisis, the United Nations World Travel Organization (UNWTO) took huge steps to stop the immediate effect that the outbreak had on the travel and tourism industry. It called upon governments from all around the world to place the recovery of the travel industry among their first priorities after the pandemic was over. It also strongly collaborated with the World Health Organization (WHO) and followed the health guidelines issued by the WHO to minimise the impact of lockdowns on the travel industry.

The World Travel and Tourism Council also suggested that governments from around the globe take basic measures to save the travel industry. These measures included simplification of visas, relaxation of unnecessary travel barriers, reduction of travel taxes, and an increase in the allotted budget for the promotion of the respective tourism bodies.

What Happened to Tourism and Hospitality Post Covid-19

Despite all the measures that were taken to hoist the travel industry back on its feet, we were all faced with an important question: Where to from here? Even if the lockdown had been lifted in April-May 2020, as originally planned, the travel industry would have lost three months' worth of business. This major revenue cut was a huge blow to the industry and it would require the next ten months to recover, at the very least.

However, there was a silver lining to all this after all. Paula Froelich of the *New York Post* said that the temporary halting of travel was able to bring out the industry more shining than ever. With major factories being shut down, pollution had drastically decreased, making the environment more beautiful than ever before. People were actually able to see clear skies, clean, sparkling rivers, and breathe fresh air after a very long time. This gave them the opportunity to be more thankful, mindful, and appreciative of their surroundings.

Being confined to their homes for a long period of time, people found the time to reflect and make note of the things they'd been missing in life. They realised that in pursuit of a fast-paced life, they'd forgotten to slow down and appreciate it for all that it offered. The lockdown served as a self-intervention, which increased the number of tourism enthusiasts exponentially.

One good thing that came out of this terrible crisis was the reduction of over-tourism. The selective crowd that travelled after the outbreak was enthusiastic, appreciative, and more considerate towards any travel destination they were visiting. They were also more mindful of their carbon footprint and inclined to reduce their wasteful practices, at least for some time.

In the long term, cleaner cities emerged as winners here. Because of the doubts and fears surrounding the ongoing coronavirus, people were hesitant to travel to densely populated areas, which gave smaller and cleaner destinations an edge over other tourist places. Also, local destinations experienced a huge rise in tourism as they were affordable, closer to home, and relatively comfortable.

For the four and a half long decades that have I been in the industry, observing and understanding how things actually are,

I have realised that being hopeful and preparing yourself for the long run is essential for the survival of any business. However, you also need to adapt to the situations if you wish to protect your business from the inevitable. Whether you own a small boutique hotel or are the general manager of an independent luxury resort or a branded luxury hotel, there are a number of things you can do to minimise the damages incurred and prepare for a return to some semblance of normality.

How We Were Able to Minimise the Damage Impact of Covid-19

This is where marketing came in. The first and most important thing hoteliers did was *to recast their marketing budget*. As a general rule of thumb, it's not a good idea to cut down on your marketing budget during times of crisis, that is, if you can afford it. Historic data has proven over time that if companies actively market themselves during a time of crisis, they typically gain higher sales and net income than those who don't. If you do have to make some cuts, make sure you do it logically and rationally.

During times of crisis, a brand must have a deep digital footprint in terms of marketing communications as this will largely determine its success. Digital marketing is faster, more effective, and less expensive than traditional marketing. A social media campaign can effectively engage your target audience for less than half of the cost of a TV or print ad. Quite wonderful, isn't it?

This is what hoteliers did during Covid. They made the most of this slow period and took it as an opportunity to rethink and *improve their marketing assets with an audit*. Those who had kept a content inventory were able to make the process of auditing go over more smoothly.

They looked for images and high-quality pieces that they then repurposed for other channels. They also explored a variety of other content that would receive the most backlinks or social shares and bring incremental traffic to their website. New calls to action and keywords were explored, internal links were added to new services, and the websites, too, were updated with fresh content.

Videos are excellent search engine optimisation fodder. Video content is versatile and can be used in several different ways. For this reason, hotels started **making promotional videos**. They were embedded into blog posts, screenshots were used as image posts, quotes from the video transcripts were used alongside images, and those quotes were even reused for media releases. These videos also became an investment of sorts, and a lot of hotels continue to use them even today.

Some hotels also started organising online webinars and live demonstrations straight from their kitchens. Sharing some common dishes and desserts with their audience went a long way in establishing direct communication between the hotels and their clients. It also became a great way to share unique content with consumers who weren't able to travel as freely as earlier.

There was yet another thing that hoteliers did that showed how they were innovatively using the situation to their advantage. Realising that their consumer had more free time on their hands, the hotel industry reached out to them and conducted *interviews using Zoom or other services. This served a twofold purpose: one, it generated engaging content for social media posts. And two, most importantly, the insights gleaned from these videos informed the hotel's marketing strategy, which helped them to plan and prepare future offerings for changing consumer perceptions.*

Responding to online reviews was also an excellent way to connect with customers. Hoteliers realised that no matter what the tone of the review, it was always a good practice to respond to it instead of letting it go unheard. For this reason, they put a comprehensive online review strategy in place, which went a long way in **building trust and generating repeat business for their brands.**

They also started training some of their employees to manage their online reviews, giving them the necessary training and tools to accomplish this task competently.

Hotels also started holding webinars to answer some of the frequently asked questions (FAQs) about their hotels, their amenities, locations, products, and services they offered. They also made FAQ videos that were pushed out on LinkedIn, YouTube, and other social media platforms, and even updated on their website eventually.

Hotels also **updated their 'Google my business'** to let their customers know if they were operating under special hours, what safety steps they had taken to avoid the spread of the virus, and what offers their customers could avail.

While it was important to consider an outreach strategy at that time, it was also important to avoid crisis-related promotions. Instead, hoteliers **got creative and thought of ways to offer reassurance, social connections, or tangible support during this crisis.** They also hosted online video spaces once a week where people could join in and have light discussions. Apart from this, SEO and online marketing also helped them build connections with people. If the customers were used to hearing from the hotel regularly through emails or other digital platforms, it was inadvisable to cut that connection during such sensitive times.

Finally, hoteliers also used this time to **take a closer look at their first-party data.** They reviewed what they knew about their customers, about prospects that didn't pick them, and things they had missed in analytics in the past. They looked for trends, both online and offline, and thought about what they could do to fix them.

As the coronavirus hit the travel and hospitality industries, there was no statistical data on how long it could take the industry to recover. Having been in the hospitality industry myself for over 40 years, I understood the difficulties that hoteliers were facing. My heart went out to them.

But I also knew that this was the time to keep our heads on straight and prepare for better days. Being hopeful definitely helped, but we had to be prepared, nevertheless. For, in the wise words of Confucius, "A man who does not plan long ahead will find trouble at his door."

Is Your Hotel an Energy Guzzler or Energy Saver?

Gone are the days when hotels could be complacent about their energy consumption or not worry about things like 'eco-friendly' measures or sustainable initiatives. With customers around the world becoming more and more aware, they're demanding that hotels step up and shoulder the responsibility of reducing energy wastage. And it doesn't hurt at all that your conservation efforts will also bear financial returns in the long run.

You wouldn't think that the words 'energy efficient' and 'hotel' would be used together in any good way. As luxurious and palatial as some of these establishments are, energy efficiency can't really be an achievable goal, right? It might be natural to follow that train of thought, but things are actually quite different at the ground level.

Eco-friendly existence and a more conscientious way of travelling and living are gaining preference among people. As a result, hotels are becoming more and more conscious of their responsibility towards the planet. There has been a concerted effort to reduce wastage, and given that power consumption tends to go through the roof in hotels, they have turned their attention to making their properties energy efficient. Not only does this pull in travellers who stand by energy conservation and eco-friendly practices, but hotels, too, can make significant financial savings in the long run, making it a win-win situation for everyone involved.

Let me clarify here that you don't have to go in for a grand retrofit project to kick-start your energy savings initiative. There are simple, yet highly effective tweaks you can make within your property to create a green hotel. Intrigued? Let's find out how.

Upgrade Your Lighting Solutions

The first thing you notice when you walk into a hotel are the number of lights that are switched on in the property—all through the day! It only stands to reason that you would begin your energy conservation efforts here.

The very first thing you should do is swap out the traditional, energy-draining light bulbs for their LED counterparts. Old-school bulbs use up to 80% of electricity to produce light. LED bulbs can bring this consumption down to just 15%. Moreover, these light bulbs last a lot longer, which means you have to replace them less often. And that's yet another way of cutting down on expenses.

Next up, look at all the areas in your hotel where lights are left on throughout the day. I am talking about hallways, common rooms, storage areas, and staff rooms that are kept lit 24 hours a day. That's a criminal waste of electricity!

The solution? Switch to motion sensor lights. The lights turn on when you're in or around the room; otherwise, they stay switched off. This simple upgrade can not only bring down your energy bills but also increase the lifespan of your lighting system.

Optimise Your HVAC System

There's no denying that the HVAC system plays a very important role in moderating the temperature indoors, but you can't also ignore the fact that its energy consumption can very easily go through the roof. Most hotels don't assess their requirements before getting an HVAC system installed. Or once installed, they ignore its care and maintenance. Get professionals on the job. Let them study the layout of your hotel—rooms, hallways, restaurants et al—and recommend a suitable solution for you.

But don't depend on your HVAC system alone for heating and cooling solutions. Pay close attention to windows and wall insulation as well. They're easy to overlook, but did you know that with proper insulation, you can prevent heat loss during winters and stay cool during summers? Thus, you will spend less energy and money on heating and cooling your property throughout the year.

Don't Ignore the Kitchen

A hotel kitchen functions round the clock, serving breakfast, lunch, brunch, snacks, dinner, and a host of drinks and beverages to its guests. The commercial appliances in there are bound to be energy guzzlers.

If you haven't already, upgrade to energy appliances that use both less power and water. Some of them also have programmable software that puts the appliances into energy conservation mode when they're not being used. The ventilation system should also be serviced and upgraded in a timely manner to regulate the temperature in the kitchen.

Consider Key Card Climate Control in Guest Rooms

Guest rooms account for 30% of the energy consumption in a hotel. Any energy-saving plan you have in a hotel cannot ignore them. In addition to LED light bulbs and a more efficient HVAC system, you should also introduce a key card climate control.

The principle is quite simple: When the guest is out of their room, the HVAC functions in 'economy' mode, which reduces energy consumption by 60%. But the moment he uses his key card to enter the room, the HVAC switches to 'occupied' mode and starts heating or cooling the space at optimum capacity. This is a great way of reducing energy consumption in your hotel without inconveniencing the guests in any way.

Energy conservation doesn't necessarily mean overhauling every single fitting in your hotel and replacing it with something hi-tech and expensive. Simple measures can go a long in way reducing power wastage and helping you move closer to your environment-friendly goals. Plan the upgrade in phases if you can't afford to go all out now. Taking tiny steps towards planned changes is still better than not doing anything at all. And with each upgrade, you'll start seeing noticeable differences in no time at all.

So get started on making your hotel energy efficient. Your guests, the planet, and your budget will all thank you for it!

Restoring Loyalty Programs: Drive in More Customers and Boost Your ROI

Today, when customers are smart and more vigilant of their preferences and needs, it is time to restore your hotel loyalty programs if you already have them. From guest appreciation to incremental revenue, loyalty schemes work in favour of customers as well as the hotel.

According to an article in the *Harvard Business Review*, titled 'Roaring Out of Recession', organisations that are able to master the difficult, yet essential, balance between cost-cutting to survive today and investing to grow tomorrow are able to survive a recession. But that is true in general scenarios, too. Those who can figure out a combination of defensive and offensive moves for their company have the highest probability—37%—of standing out in the crowd. Further, reinvesting in building customer loyalty amplifies the return on investment (ROI) of prior budget allocations to customer-facing initiatives.

While we know loyalty programs are important, how to augment the efficiency of these programs can be challenging. We already know that the bottom line of differentiated loyalty programs lies in an excellent customer experience that anticipates and integrates their personalised needs as a priority by the hotel. Further, in assessing the brand loyalty of travellers, we have to understand how attitudes and behaviours change between two kinds of customers—business travellers and leisure travellers. For example, both business (84%) and leisure (79%) travellers say that the most valued redemption benefit is night stays. Room upgrades come in a distant second for business travellers, whereas leisure travellers like to redeem loyalty points for airfares.

Interestingly, when you look at the data based on age groups, a different picture emerges. While hotel nights are still the number one choice for all travellers, 36% of millennial travellers (30 years and above) chose upgrades as their second preferred reward, compared with only 16% of other younger travellers.

What can be inferred from this is that business travellers value loyalty benefits over leisure travellers. And that is why nearly 60% of leisure travellers do not redeem their loyalty points annually. This could be because of the following reasons.

- When young leisure travellers are on a strict travel budget, they usually prefer economical options like bed-and-breakfasts and hostels over traditional options like five-star or luxurious hotels.

- On a business trip, the traveller prefers the comfort and amenities of a branded hotel, but when it comes to leisure vacations, he looks for experiences to take back home rather than freebies from the hotel.

So, What Can Hotels Do to Restore Their Brand Loyalty among All Kinds of Customers?

1. **Redefine customer loyalty programs:** So far, the loyalty benefits meant extra discounts on the final bill, room upgrades, or loyalty points for their next stay. For very long, travellers were happy with these little incentives, but it doesn't work anymore.

   The new travellers are more aware and want value for every penny. Hotels can engage them by using customer referrals, social media reviews, or constructive customer feedback forms in exchange for a complimentary dinner, recreational activities like a spa session or movie tickets, or a bag of goodies at the end of their stay.

2. **Refocus on customer preference:** Loyalty membership databases are already overflowing with customer information like demographics, travel preferences, and average time and money they spend at the hotel. Mining this data will likely produce an understanding of discrete customer segments with distinct service preferences.

    For example, if business travellers are more likely to enjoy your loyalty benefits, it will be smart to refocus your loyalty program towards them. You can offer regular business travellers free pick-up and drop services to and from the airport. Or, you could have a co-working space on your property and offer its services to business travellers at a lower rate. Or offer them a bottle of wine at the end of a long day.

3. **Reinvest in capabilities and infrastructure:** Hotels should build the technology, talent, training, and infrastructure to deliver differentiated customer experiences that extend beyond on-premise experiences. Technology, especially, can be a powerful tool to engage customers through all stages of travel—planning, doing, and sharing.

    Creating personalised experiences like an efficient and courteous check-in process (mobile check-in), acknowledgement of program membership and participation, and welcome emails from hotel managers work like magic.

In the current-day scenario, the idea of loyalty programs is to look beyond convoluted rewards systems and offer actual value to customers. Loyalty programs are beneficial to both parties. While you want people who enjoy your property to return as often as possible, your customers would love an extra incentive to do so. In addition, the more consistently you communicate the benefits and appreciation for regular guests, the more they will feel like you are creating an experience especially customised for them. And when your guest feels valued, the other things, too, fall into place easily.

Are you off to follow your dream of having a hotel of your own? Congratulations. But before you take the plunge, have you kept the basics of such an investment in mind?

Boutique hotels are all the rage these days as more and more travellers are showing a preference for smaller and more private properties to stay in while on vacation. This is probably why there's an upsurge in investments in boutique hotels. Given the change in travel trends, it just makes a lot of financial sense.

If you've been entertaining thoughts of investing in a boutique hotel of your own, wonderful! You're certainly on your way to making a good business decision. But it's important for you not to rush into it. There are a lot of considerations you should be mindful of before you take the plunge. Here are the top ones that come to mind

Start by Giving It a Second Thought

The life of a hotelier has its appeal for sure—doing up a cosy property in a charming location, entertaining high-flying guests, living a life of leisure as you sit by the pool and sip your favourite drink... it's the greatest advertising poster there could be.

But don't get swept away by such sentiments. Every investment has to be made on practical considerations, and you can't lose sight of that. There's nothing wrong with wanting to live your dreams, but you should be prepared for all the demands that your dream will make on you. The hospitality sector may be about providing the perfect getaway experience, but running a boutique hotel is anything but a holiday.

Have a USP and Know Your Audience

I've come across several hoteliers who pour themselves into the details of what their establishment is going to look like. However, they have no clue about how to arrive at their unique selling proposition (USP) or how they plan on driving people to their hotel. This eventually leads to a lot of trouble when it comes to getting their business off the ground. With poor footfall during the initial period, revenue takes a hit, which in turn affects profitability, not to mention morale.

When setting up a hotel, don't just think about details like location, interiors, the design of the rooms, and the food and services you're going to offer. You've also got to think very carefully about how you're going to set yourself apart. What's your unique identity? And how are you going to market your services?

Don't forget that the hospitality industry is extremely competitive. You are one among the many boutique hotels out there, and only a strong USP, backed by a stronger marketing strategy, will set you apart.

Do Thorough Market Research

Research lays a strong foundation for your new business, and stepping into it without doing your due diligence is the easiest way to see your investment do a nosedive.

So what are the things you need to research?

Your audience, to begin with. Who are the travellers you're targeting? What is their demographic profile? What are they likely to be interested in? When do they travel? What kind of travel experiences do they like? All this research is key to creating a strong audience profile that you can use to guide your marketing efforts.

Then, you need to research the location the hotel is in. What kind of footfall does it receive? When does it see the most travellers? What are the sightseeing options around the hotel and within the city? Are there any local vendors you could tie up with? Any unique crafts or artists you could promote or unique experiences you could create? Looking into all these factors will bring you a better understanding of the area you'll be operating, along with its potential and its drawbacks.

Finally, research your competition. This should include everything from how much they charge to the services they're offering, the way they're managing their properties, what they've got on their menu, and the deals and discounts they're extending to their customers. While you're at it, read their online reviews and check their social media presence. And if you can, book a few days' stay in a few of the more popular hotels in the area to get a real feel of what they're offering. Closely investigating your competitors will help you learn what they're doing right while making a note of the gaps in their service that you can fill in your upcoming establishment.

There's a very popular saying that comes to my mind: "Well begun is half done." If you cover your basics before taking the plunge into becoming a hotelier, you'll find that you'll be better prepared for what lies ahead. And while we have no control over unforeseen circumstances, there's no excuse for not being prepared for common obstacles in the business. So do your homework before embarking on the journey to fulfilling your dreams. All the best!

There's no denying that food is at the heart of your restaurant, but arriving at the selection of food items that make their way onto the menu is a slow process. A lot of effort goes into designing a menu, and you should give it the thought and attention that it deserves.

A restaurant menu does a lot more than offer your guests a list of food and drinks to order from. A well-designed menu can significantly enhance guest experience and set the mood for his culinary journey from the moment he comes and sits at your table. If you're investing considerable thought and effort into designing the look and feel of your entire restaurant, don't overlook an equally important factor—the presentation of the menu. You've got to make a strong impression on your guests from the word go, but that isn't the only reason why a menu should be given due attention. It can also contribute towards designing the kitchen and the layout of the bar, which can deliver effective storage, productivity, and preparation.

If you're convinced about the importance of having a strong menu, let's look at the process of creating one.

Step 1: Put some thought into your menu concept

Every good restaurant that you've ever visited has that 'best one thing' going for it. It could be the spicy pasta, juicy steaks, fusion cuisine, or its amazing selection of desserts. Whatever it was, it stayed with you long after you'd finished your meal and left the restaurant.

To make a strong menu concept, you have to think long and hard about what your restaurant's USP will be. What will it be known for? What will set it apart from the crowd? But avoid getting too ambitious. Crowd your menu with too many things, and it will cause unnecessary clutter. Guests don't like being overwhelmed by too many choices. They prefer to decide within two minutes of picking up the menu.

Don't complicate life for them. Keep it simple and have select offerings. Make a list of items you'd like to feature in your menu. If you notice that it's running too long, narrow it down and make it more focused.

Step 2: Decide on a list of core ingredients

Once you've decided on the main concept, you have to move on to making a list of the actual ingredients that will bring the wow factor to the menu.

Why is this important? And why do you need to do it so early in the menu designing process? Simple—to figure out your supply chain.

Once you've identified the core ingredients, the next step is to figure out who your suppliers are. It stands to reason that the more exotic ingredients you have on your menu, the more limited your vendors are likely to be. On the other hand, if you're sourcing locally grown and readily available products, the supply chain will become that much easier to manage.

It's always advisable to work with what you've got. When you source from the food artisans in your area or meat from smaller, home-grown units, you not only cut down on expenses but also encourage the local community and give them business. Furthermore, working with locally available food cuts down the risk of ingredients running out of stock due to bad weather or delays in shipment, which could, in turn, throw your menu planning out of whack and leave your customers less than happy.

Step 3: It's time to do the costing

You've got your concept. You've identified the core ingredients. You've worked out the supply chain, too. Now what?

Now it's time to bring them all together and see what your menu is going to cost you and your guests!

Doing the costing is a fairly easy process. You could use a recipe management program or rely on the good old Excel sheet and enter the data at hand into it. This process allows you to analyse the portions of the menu, the ingredients associated with each item, the supplier's cost, and other related factors. This, in turn, will help you price the menu items in a way that suits your target audience and the local economy. At the same time, you will be able to work out whether there's a good balance in the pricing with regard to your competitors and how much profit you'll be making after you've factored in everything else.

This exercise (which will go through several rounds of trial and error, mind you!) is an important one and answers several important questions. Are you being too ambitious with your menu? Will your audience be able to afford you? Are you charging a lot more or less than your competitors (which might affect consumers' perception of you)? And finally, what will you be making at the end of the day for all the effort you've put in?

The final stage of the menu planning process is running a test kitchen to see if the menu items actually meet and exceed your expectations. Make it, plate it, tweak it, and bring in other people (friends, relatives, a small group of target customers) to give you feedback. Based on their reactions, modify the menu a little more before you do the final launch of your restaurant. And because you've been so thorough, I have no doubt that your menu will certainly grab everyone's attention. All the best!

There's a very popular saying, "Out of sight, out of mind." And the hotel industry is acutely aware of its relevance to their business. With the new generation of millennial travellers that are landing at their establishments, hotels must amp up their presence online to be discoverable and stay relevant.

Fun fact 1: Millennials hold more than 65% of global buying power. This means that two out of three people buying something in the world are probably millennials. Fun Fact 2: Millennials spend five hours or more on social media every day. The internet is almost like a second home to them. Fun Fact 3: Millennials love to travel and gather new experiences.

What do you get when you put all these three facts together? An alert to the hotel industry that it's high time they thought about including digital strategies in their marketing plan. Old-school marketing can no longer tide them over since they're dealing with new-age consumers who have very different personalities, preferences, and buying patterns. If you're not digitally active, you are practically invisible to the millennial audience.

So, if you're hoping not to fade into oblivion and you'd like to continue being relevant to the current generation of travellers, it's time to take your hotel online.

Invest in a Good Website

When it comes to online presence, most hotels believe that registering with online travel agencies (OTAs) like MakeMyTrip,

Trivago, and TripAdvisor is enough. However, several online users are in the habit of visiting the hotel website, looking for either more information or better deals.

Having a good website allows you to tell your hotel's story your way. You can elaborate on the services you offer, any special packages you have, and exclusive experiences that you're hosting. On your website, you also have the luxury of showcasing your property in a flattering manner and can keep updating the gallery with new photos. Furthermore, an active website also boosts your search engine optimisation (SEO), and in the long run, it could bring in a substantial amount of sales and leads as well, thereby reducing your dependency on OTAs.

Manage Your Online Reputation

If there's one thing that everyone knows within the hospitality industry, it's that reputation is everything. Word of mouth can bring in more leads than all other marketing strategies put together. However, one bad review is enough to wreck your business.

When there's so much riding on your reputation, you should have a separate strategy dedicated to it, which should ideally be two-fold:

a) Encourage customers to share positive reviews about their stay and experiences. Incentivise this process, if necessary, by giving discounts, room upgrades, or additional perks and services to your guests. The process should be ongoing, and customer testimonials should be shared on your website and social media profiles.

b) Actively monitor what others are saying about you online on various platforms, like blogs, forums, and social media. Acknowledge every kind word said about you and address any negative reviews that you may come across. Do not make the mistake of ignoring something you don't like. Instead, apologise and use the opportunity to alleviate any issues that might inconvenience future guests.

If you stand by and do nothing, you are letting others control the narrative about you. It's *your* reputation and you should be on top of it at all times.

Give Email Marketing a Try

A lot of people believe that email marketing is an outdated marketing technique. And yet, it still remains one of the most effective, not to mention affordable, ways of staying in touch with your audience. In this fast-moving world where travellers have all the options in the world at their fingertips, out of sight is almost as good as out of mind. Emails go a long way in increasing your recall value and even help to bring in repeat customers.

To ensure the success of your email marketing campaign, here are a few tips you can start with:

- In your eagerness to be visible, never spam your customers. If you pop up in their inbox with annoying frequency, you'll find that they'll be just as quick to unsubscribe from your list.

- Avoid sending generic content. Do proper segmentation of your customers and design mailers for the different audiences you're targeting. You cannot be sending the same mailer to, let's say, an adventure enthusiast and a family man.

- Design the mailer well. Do not settle for mediocre design or copy; use the mailer to convey real value to your target audience. Give them a compelling reason to click on your email and go through it.

If you take the right approach, email marketing can prove to be a great and effective tool in your marketing arsenal.

In this day and age, there's absolutely no excuse for you not to go digital, especially when the modern generation of travellers is so tech-savvy. It's time to reinvent yourself and go with the flow. If you refuse to do so, you're practically handing over your business to your competitors. And I am sure you have no desire to do that!

In-Room Entertainment: Catering to 21st-century Travellers

With the change in viewing habits and the use of personal devices among today's generation, hoteliers are facing challenges in providing truly integrated in-room entertainment experiences. However, this scenario is improving drastically with technology and innovation. Hotels can do more than provide a choice between cable TV channels or watching content on their personal devices. They can offer their guests the freedom to be in control of their hotel stay experience.

Earlier, in-room facilities were simple. A telephone to call room service, a TV to enjoy cable shows, and rented movies you could choose from were all a hotel had to offer. Guests, too, never bothered about entertainment facilities that much. However, the expectations of modern hotel guests have changed drastically in recent years. For them, just a comfortable place to stay is no longer enough. Today's digitally connected travellers want to enjoy the same kind of connectivity at a hotel as they do at home. Even if your guest is using the room as a place to only eat and sleep, the time they spend in the room relaxing will invariably involve browsing the net, streaming videos, or listening to music. Such dependence on personal gadgets and a hike in on-demand entertainment are transforming guests' expectations.

With that in mind, let's explore the growing in-room entertainment facilities and how hoteliers can implement these technologies in their hotels.

Easy Access to Personal Devices

On-demand videos in the room and pay-per-view have become things of the past. Now, travellers across generations prefer streaming on their own devices, which means a frictionless online experience is the key to guest satisfaction. A hotel that offers seamless connectivity, accommodating the usage of multiple mobile devices per room while ensuring good bandwidth at the lounging facility is a star in a traveller's eyes.

A survey conducted by Openkey shows that 88% of hotel guests expect device charging ports and 98% expect high-speed Wi-Fi. While installing high-quality plug points is easy, high-speed and glitch-free internet connections need some work.

The basic calculation is based on three primary points:

– How many guest rooms are there in the hotel?

– How much square footage is the common area?

– What is expected from a typical guest in terms of the bandwidth that they will require to be able to stream devices or connect to the services that you offer?

Generally, a big hotel with 100 to 400 rooms deploys a 500-megabyte bandwidth system. Similarly, a property with 500 plus rooms needs a full gigabyte bandwidth to ensure smooth streaming.

Personal Content and Streaming Services

In a survey conducted by Nielson, over 66% of hotel guests prefer watching video-on-demand on a bigger screen than on a mobile device. Taking this into account, in-room entertainment is undoubtedly going to revolve around the hotel TV. As internet-enabled smart TVs have become prevalent in homes, guests come to your hotel expecting to stream their favourite Netflix or Amazon Prime shows on the in-room TVs, too.

Similarly, with the boom in internet-based music platforms like Spotify, guests would love to play their music via the in-room TV Bluetooth speakers. This is where streaming services can add massive value to guest satisfaction. Rather than being confined to a small screen, letting guests cast content from a personal device to the in-room TV makes for a far less restricted and more enjoyable online and in-room entertainment experience.

In order to meet customers' demands for instant and more personalised services, hotels are investing in comprehensive guest room entertainment solutions. It is available in the form of content casting and voice-activated in-room smart devices. These devices allow guests to cast virtually any kind of content from personal devices onto larger TV screens, including Netflix and Hulu and social media platforms such as Facebook or Twitter. Unlike televisions that provide such services only via preinstalled apps, these devices steer clear of privacy concerns that arise when entering personal login details. These devices are programmed such that guests can delete personal data at any time or details get erased automatically when the guests check out.

Redefining the In-Room Entertainment Experience

As dependence on personal digital devices grows, in-room entertainment is defined by what your guests bring with them. A hotel's role lies in how well they can enhance the experience of guests using their devices during their stay, whether it's for entertainment or work.

Super-fast Wi-Fi connections, casting services, and voice-activated devices are no longer luxuries. They have become a hardwired expectation, affecting your business and its reputation.

If expectations are not met, you might lose business and face backlash on social media. After all, seamless connectivity has become a basic necessity in today's fast-paced life.

The ongoing evolution of consumer technology means that guests are now accustomed to a high degree of personalised experience when it comes to their in-room entertainment demands. They expect the same level of quality regardless of where they stay or what kind of hotel they check into. Modern internet-enabled devices not only completely fulfil this growing demand but also give an opportunity to incorporate other satisfaction-enhancing amenities. For example, in-room television can be used to watch a movie and order hotel services. How amazing is that!

In a nutshell, for today's travellers, in-room entertainment holds great importance, just like any other amenity on your property. With internet-enabled and voice-controlled devices, your guests look forward to having the same comfort and quality as they enjoy in their homes. At the same time, the more you offer, the better it is for your business. Things get even better when guests are able to take control over their own hotel stay experience and interact with amenities in a way that is more convenient and in line with their preferences for faster service. Entertainment autonomy and an 'office' away from the office are what your existing and future guests are looking for. Understanding these changing demands and expectations and investing in the right technology are crucial for gaining a competitive edge in the years to come.

Changing Sales, Marketing, and Customer Engagement Through Technology in the Hotel Industry

Grabbing customers' attention used to be a time-intensive but simple task in the past. Directory listings, radio, and print ads were the most popular and preferred mediums for targeting customers. On the other hand, customers also had limited choices. Direct telephone bookings or contacting travel agents were the only ways to book a room in a hotel. However, the internet changed everything, and the evolution in IT brought a paradigm shift to sales, marketing, and customer engagement in the hotel industry.

Today, information technology governs every industry, and the hospitality industry is no exception. Travel portals and apps have enabled customers to book rooms through a few clicks. Nothing seems far-fetched, and nothing is impossible now. Hotels are trying their best to impress customers by providing them with the convenience of mobile room keys, personalised interaction terminals, and whatnot. However, some hotels still struggle with ineffective customer engagement due to a lack of coordination and technology in their sales and marketing operations.

The solution to this problem is in technology as it has become a necessity today. Ensuring effective customer engagement by streamlining sales and marketing operations is achievable by using the right tools and techniques.

Here is an overview of how technology is improving sales, marketing, and customer engagement operations in the hotel industry.

Technology for Effective Customer Engagement

The internet is making a substantial impact on both existing and potential customers, especially in the tourism and hospitality industry. A hotel that has successfully created a positive image about its services is usually the first choice for travel enthusiasts. True customer experiences through reviews, testimonies, and blogs can build trust in a hotel's treatment of its guests.

AI-enabled chatbot terminals are becoming more popular day by day. Many hotel groups have such terminals at their front desks, lobbies, and luxury suites. These terminals allow guests to interact with the staff without any fuss. The guests can access the central system either through their phones or via terminals. On one hand, the technology condenses verbal communication between guests and the staff, and on the other, it opens up a passive dialogue with more clarity and with minimal conflicts.

However, both existing and potential customers should feel they are being forced to interact. For instance, a simple website notification must contain both 'accept' and 'decline' buttons. It gives customers the freedom of choice and creates a positive image of the business. Similarly, the check-in/check-out terminals should offer a smooth user experience. Asking for too much personal information or taking too long to respond may cause all your efforts to go in vain.

Technology for Data Collection and Analysis

A centralised system for information sharing, assigning tasks to the staff, or acting on guests' requests makes things quite easy. Moreover, the system can also collect and process vast amounts of customer data. The data refers to specific customer information, including their preferences, past visits, and interactions at various points of sale.

The information can help hoteliers understand their guests' preferences along with the weak points in their processes. Although analysing such vast amounts of data is not easy, the system itself can be of great help in this aspect. It intelligently segments for the managers to identify actionable points and further analyse the data.

Predictive analysis is another aspect where smart systems use AI as their primary framework. Smart systems are capable of running intelligent operations such as data analysis, data processing, and deriving insights on their own. The system can identify the patterns, which makes it easy for decision-makers to study the data for forecasting and building marketing strategies.

Data-Driven Marketing and Sales

Modern marketing operations are data-driven. The responsibilities of marketing managers are not limited to ideation and conceptualisation. They need to be aware of market trends and customer behaviour patterns to build robust marketing strategies for both online and offline interactions. Data-driven marketing helps hotels deliver personalised customer experiences by conveying the right message at the right time to the right people. This is equally applicable to sales as a carefully designed marketing strategy will certainly help sales personnel in conveying the right products/services to guests.

A data-driven approach towards marketing also enables marketers to gain clarity about their target audience. Marketers should know about the platforms and engagement opportunities that could be profitable. In addition, data-driven marketing can also be helpful in effective product development. A clear understanding of customers' needs is crucial in creating the ideal products/services that ultimately improve guests' experiences.

Technology for Customer Satisfaction

This is one of the most critical and tricky aspects of the hotel industry. Sincere hoteliers try to deliver top-quality services to their guests, but there are times when someone commits a mistake and the guest immediately posts a negative review online. It is not the practicality of a service that matters. Instead, customisation and levels of compassion for the needs of guests matter the most. There is no absolute solution to this problem, but hoteliers can try and improve customer satisfaction through automated responses and personalised services.

Automating time-intensive operations is one way to achieve guest satisfaction. For instance, guests can use phone check-in and check-out through the hotel's apps that are integrated into the central management system. Sending digital room keys to guests' phones is another scenario where both the hotel and guests don't have to worry about lost keycards and theft.

Adding an element of personalisation to the services can also deliver exceptional customer satisfaction. The staff can greet their guests on their birthdays or anniversaries. The central system keeps track of such information, and it can update the staff about the same. Such small gestures may not seem important, but birthdays and anniversaries are special days for people. Wishing your guests on such dates shows caring, which will ultimately reflect in their feedback.

The hotel industry is going through a paradigm shift where technology is changing traditional norms. Both hotels and guests prefer AI-based automated operations due to their specific perks. Hotels get to improve and automate their workflow while guests enjoy the freedom of remote interaction and multiple choices. However, the decision-makers have to carefully manage their sales and marketing operations by segregating the roles and responsibilities of each department for efficient management.

"Your most unhappy customers are
your greatest source of learning."

– Bill Gates

The Curious Case of Hotels Acquiring Boutique Properties

The popularity of boutique hotels among travellers has led to an ever-increasing number of acquisitions in the hospitality industry. However, corporations are struggling to adapt their business models in a way that preserves the individuality of these hotels while also maximising profits.

Boutique hotels have become a favourite among travellers due to their upscale accommodations and unique selling points. Especially in the Instagram age, the inherent 'shareability' of boutique hotels attracts travellers from all over the world in their quest for distinctive experiences and social media likes.

What Makes Boutique Hotels Different?

Boutique hotels started as a few one-of-a-kind properties designed around the preferences of Gen X travellers who want more than a typical hotel stay. This has turned into a full-blown trend among millennials, which has taken the hospitality industry by storm.

The crowd that flocks to boutique hotels finds something there that is missing in conventional hotels, such as:

- Personalised attention to their needs

- Strong individuality and representation of local culture through theme-based architecture and decor

- A cosy experience due to the intimate size of the hotel, usually around 10 to 100 rooms

Hence, boutique hotels receive heavy footfall and have become go-to properties for having a memorable trip. Their massive demand and high ADRs have led to high revenues despite their limited number of rooms. However, the maintenance costs of these hotels can be quite high, and the profit margins may not be as high as hoteliers expect.

Still, the rising demand has awoken corporations' interest in capitalising on this trend. They are now looking for ways to acquire boutique hotels and make them more profitable. However, standard corporate behaviour can make hoteliers lose sight of what makes boutique hotels so sought after and turn them into slightly quirky yet run-of-the-mill hotels. If this happens, guests who frequented the establishment might lose interest and stop frequenting it.

What Should Hoteliers Do to Prevent This?

- **Protect the secret ingredient**

  The most important thing to remember is that boutique hotels are all about the quirk that sets them apart. It might be a specific motif they follow in their decor or a cause they support that resonates with travellers. It could also be a niche service they offer, a specific clientele they might be catering to, or any unique trait that gives the hotel a distinct personality.

  Whatever this secret ingredient may be, hoteliers must ensure they preserve the idiosyncratic nature of boutique hotels, or the demand will fall over time.

  At the same time, hotel chains must look after their interests and look for ways to improve the profitability of the hotels they're acquiring. Therefore, once the organisation is aware of the acquired hotel's secret ingredient, it should focus on strategising for its growth.

The biggest benefits of a hotel chain acquiring a boutique hotel are the additional working capital and the industry expertise it brings in. These add a fresh business-like perspective to the boutique model and create new opportunities, such as more resources for market research and business growth. Since the end goal is to increase profitability, hoteliers should not overprotect the property or fear experimenting with new ways to conduct day-to-day operations.

- **Hire advisors**

To maintain this precarious balance, hoteliers should hire industry experts who have a deep understanding of the local culture along with the theme of the boutique hotel. Hoteliers should not restrict themselves to advisors within the hospitality industry as individuals who demonstrate a creative background from different industries will most certainly help them find innovative solutions.

Moreover, such individuals would have extensive experience that will allow them to figure out weaknesses that hoteliers might miss otherwise. This could be a shortcoming in their operational strategy, a product that might be eating up revenue but not generating any, or something as simple as incorrect market positioning. Once these weaknesses have been outlined, they can then work towards removing them in a strategic manner that does not disrupt the hotel's personality.

- **Prepare for low profit margins**

Lastly, the corporations must remember that boutique hotels run in a league of their own and have vastly different business models. The RevPAR of specialty hotels might be high, but the GOPPAR usually does not follow. Generating profit in the short term is secondary to ensuring profits in the long term. Therefore, they should prepare for the low profit margins that come with running such types of hotels, at least initially.

The space for boutique hotels is ripe for innovation, making it the best time for established hotel chains to step in. All hotels need to do is carefully plan their goals and strategies, and they might create a profitable venture from a trend.

Hotel Property Management Systems: Undeniably Critical for Your Business

Managing a property in today's dynamic scenario takes a lot more than you can imagine. Hotel property management systems play a vital role in supporting the management in keeping your business up and running. It offers hoteliers the power to improve operating efficiency and deliver exceptional guest experiences.

The modern hospitality landscape is quite different from what it used to be. Customers expect hotels to be efficient and pick up the pace with their daily operations and processes to meet the demands of their clientele. A hotel property management system (PMS) can be of great help in such a scenario.

Modern PMSs are equipped with cutting-edge technology that helps hotels to automate and streamline daily operations and improve efficiency for maximising customer satisfaction and revenue. From booking to final billing, PMS enables both small and multi-city hotels to comfortably manage their front desk operations, internal workflow, and customer data

Here's how PMS assists hoteliers in running their business successfully:

Structured solutions: By automating basic functions, such as information sharing and sending alerts, PMS creates opportunities for the staff to serve their guests better. Implementation of a hotel PMS means that you can reduce manual work to a great extent. In some cases, it reduces or even eliminates the time spent on lengthy tasks and operations, allowing hoteliers to focus on guests and their needs.

Transparent communication: Clear communication between different teams of a hotel is essential. It helps them work in sync and serve guests optimally. PMS provides scope for direct communication among all the teams, ensuring effective and efficient operations. Most importantly, it saves time and offers guests an improved and more personalised experience.

Sophisticated revenue tactics: By keeping track of key performance indicators (KPIs), PMS allows hoteliers to implement effective data-driven revenue management strategies. Tracking indicators such as average daily rate (ADR), revenue per available room (RevPAR), and gross operating profit per available room (GOPPAR) help hoteliers understand revenue flow and performance while facilitating better business decisions.

While these are a few points on how PMS helps in the efficient functioning of a hotel, here's how it supports the hotel staff in daily operations.

Front desk staff: Using a PMS, a hotel's front desk staff can streamline the reservation process. Right from accepting bookings (coming via walk-ins, travel agents, or OTAs) and assigning rooms to sending out confirmation emails to the guests, everything is just a few clicks away. The same goes for booking cancellations/modifications and room upgrades.

Help staff in guest registration: Apart from recording guest details, such as full name, type (FIT or corporate), gender, nationality, and contact details, a PMS also records guests' preferences on aspects such as food, payment modes, and room booked during their last stay. Such details can help you understand and serve them better in the future.

Help staff in night audit through MIS: For night audits, PMS automatically posts room tariffs and taxes on guests' folios by confirming and reconciling the final balance of the entire day's transactions. Similarly, you can track, evaluate, and determine the performance of your business from monthly, quarterly, and annual management information system (MIS) reports. PMS also provides accurate and comprehensive statistical data for forecasting and budgeting so that businesses can offer services at competitive prices.

Housekeeping staff: The standard of housekeeping plays a vital role in ensuring guest satisfaction. The front desk staff can mark rooms as 'vacant' post-checkout on PMS and send an alert to the housekeeping department. Similarly, the housekeeping staff can mark the room as 'available to occupy' after cleaning. This results in faster check-in and check-out for guests along with a seamless flow of information between the departments.

Point of sales (POS) staff: Guests don't just stay in their rooms as they often use the bar, restaurant, gym, spa, and other facilities as well. There are different points of sale (POS) that can share information about the customers and deliver a tailor-made experience. In such a scenario, POS staff can update a guest's POS charges/non-room charges directly to their tabs. This way, the guest can pay the total bill in one go while checking out. PMS and POS integration helps save time and avoid billing errors at the same time.

Increasingly disruptive innovations and advanced technologies have changed the way hoteliers run their business. From artificial intelligence to robots and virtual reality, advancements in PMS software will further help hotels multiply their revenue and serve their guests better.

"When you acknowledge, as you must, that there is no such thing as perfect food, only the idea of it, then the real purpose of striving toward perfection becomes clear: to make people happy, that is what cooking is all about."

– Thomas Keller

The Hospitality Industry Needs to Make Mobiles a Priority

In this digital age, users now expect all products and services to be accessible to them via mobile apps or platforms and have formed an aversion to direct contact with customer service reps. Due to this phenomenon, it is a priority for the hospitality industry to focus on mobiles for providing services and promoting themselves. Here's an update on the current mobile trends and what hotels can do to make the best of these.

While all industries rely on creating a good customer experience and providing quality products and services, if we had to pinpoint one industry that most heavily relies on this feature of customer service, it would be the hospitality industry. By providing services that are not up to the mark and consequently losing the goodwill of their customers, hotels and resorts face a huge possibility of failure as their success depends on fulfilling the demands of their guests, in other words, being as 'hospitable' as possible.

In such a scenario, it is no wonder that the industry needs to adapt to all new trends that come up in this fast-paced, technologically-led environment we live in. And no one can contest that mobile apps and technology are one of the biggest trends today, especially for service-oriented industries. With the 'app generation', automation is rising, and users want everything accessible through their phones, not just because of the ease of use but also because of the discomfort that comes with direct interaction today. There are now apps for everything, from ordering food to calling a cab, and users are not used to making calls or having face-to-face interactions anymore.

Indeed, anything that involves personal interaction has a chance of scaring customers away due to this resistance to unwanted social contact. Thus, it is necessary for the hospitality industry to look after this need and provide alternate methods involving the least amount of effort so that they do not lose customers who would otherwise make use of their services. In an example of such automation, hotels increasingly started to automate the TVs provided in rooms to make in-hotel services and activities—such as ordering room service, scheduling spa sessions, controlling room devices like ACs, lights, etc., and even checking out of the room—accessible to users without having to call reception. This still leaves the booking and check-in services for consideration, a space that was filled by booking services and aggregators that let users browse and book rooms by filtering their search on apps and websites.

However, this presents a problem to hotels in that users have less chance of becoming brand loyal when presented with other options while booking, making it easy for them to stray to another hotel that might be cheaper or offering a better deal.

Dedicated Mobile Apps

Many major hotels have come up with rewards programs and dedicated apps that offer users points and advantages for loyalty to their brands. Some hotels have taken it a step further and capitalised on this trend of apps by creating their own apps for booking and payments. Still, a need exists for further innovation. Hotels are experimenting with different ways mobiles can help them entice customers to use their services by making things as simple and painless for their guests as possible. One up-and-coming trend is that of the mobile key, which enables customers to use a digital key available on their mobiles to enter their rooms without having to keep track of their key cards.

In fact, the best thing for hotels right now is to create one single app for their hotel that does everything, offering end-to-end services from checking in to booking hotel services to checking out. Major hotel chains have already started implementing this model, and it's now time for other brands to also jump on this bandwagon before they get left behind.

It is critical for hotels to make the mobile experience for users as seamless and simple as possible, keeping their apps free of complicated processes and dead ends to make sure users do not have to put in much effort to understand what they have to do, or they are likely to give up on that app and go elsewhere. They must anticipate the users' needs and ensure that features matching those needs are accessible on the mobile app as well ensuring that the app is easy to operate. Another priority is to ensure that, while the website should be optimised for mobile browsers, it leads directly to the mobile app so that customers are less likely to book with another service having already downloaded the app. Even if they do not end up booking, this will enable push notifications to keep the brand in users' minds and nudge them towards various deals from time to time.

Above all, they must make sure that both the design and copy are simple, effective, and in sync with the message they are trying to convey to their users. Apps that are less effective are not likely to convince users to utilise such services as those offered through the app.

Mobile Marketing

Whether the hotel has an app or not, mobile marketing should nevertheless be a priority. And it is not just their own apps hotels need to focus on but social networking apps, too. Platforms like Facebook, X, Instagram, etc., have become a very important part of a user's travel decisions, especially with the rise of Instagram influencers.

Too many hotels focus on merely pushing ads on these platforms and neglect the power of organic marketing while others create content upon content but neglect to push them with paid advertising. They must strike a balance between the two to properly market their services to the public. What is most important for the hospitality industry is to focus on reaching out to their audience through content and paid marketing, then focus on maintaining relationships with this audience by not only providing quality content but also responding to their feedback, queries, etc., and interact with them using social networking apps. In an age where guest reviews and feedback are front and centre in the customers' research while making booking decisions, the best marketing advice for hotels is to focus on creating positive interactions with their guests.

This can be through interacting with them in the comments sections of Facebook and Instagram, responding to their posts and reviews, collaborating with Instagram influencers, and even interacting with them through chatbots or messaging platforms like WhatsApp or Facebook Messenger.

It is clear that mobiles have become a priority in the industry, and rightfully so. It is safe to assume that there might come a day when the customer experience will be fully mobile-based, and hotels must start moving towards that stage.

Lobbies: The New Hangout Place in a Hotel

Gone are the days when guests would stay holed up in their hotel rooms. They now prefer to move out and mingle with others. This is exactly why hotels are bringing about a change in designing their lobbies.

When you think of a hotel lobby, what's the first thing that comes to your mind? Deserted areas meant only for basic things like checking in, checking out, and waiting around? Spaces that play ghostly-sounding piano music while hotel staff move around like shadows? Although that's been the general perception for a very long time, the picture has changed in the past few years.

Sherry Turkle, a professor of social studies at the Massachusetts Institute of Technology (MIT), has researched the

relationship between technology and social interaction and says that there is a concept of a 'third space' in sociology. Relating it to hotels, she says, "It isn't home, but it isn't someplace we don't belong. A hotel... is such a place." Lately, hotels have been banking on this very concept to make the lobbies a place for people to mingle, network, and interact.

Noah Silverman, Marriott International's chief development officer for full-service hotels in North America, compared hotel lobbies of yore to bowling alleys of marble, which almost seemed like pass-through spaces. But that has changed. Hotels, especially hospitality giants like Marriott and Hilton, as well as their competitors, are investing more and more to transform lobbies into hangout spots.

The Shift Among Millennials

While technology has mostly been a boon for various kinds of advancements, it has also been a bane as far as human interactions are concerned. People, especially those belonging to the younger generation, are almost always seen immersed in their phones or tablets, clicking selfies, playing online games, and basically participating in virtual conversations and isolated.

The situation among millennial guests is shifting, though, with a majority of them wanting to hang out in the lobby, even if all they're doing is working on their laptops. Although this shift has led to a reduction in the size of individual rooms, it has also caused the inclusion of bright and airy lobbies, communal areas with scenic views, and ample pod seats, to attract more new-age travellers.

Lobbies as Mingling Spaces

Ian Schrager, the co-founder of the 1970s hotspot Studio 54, and later, boutique hotels, is among the many hoteliers wishing to use the comfort Millennials have with open-space mingling at work and home to their advantage. Just like private cubicles are being replaced with open-plan offices, and traditional home offices are transitioning to laptops on the tables of local cafes, giant in-room hotel desks are changing into shared workspaces. With Wi-Fi being easily available in lobbies and charging stations being accessible in almost every nook and cranny, guests prefer to step out of their rooms into a more open space to complete their work while striking conversations with fellow travellers.

Earlier, you could just order room service; now, you might have to walk down to the lobby, the restaurant, or the bar to have a meal or grab a drink. Hotels are incorporating all sorts of culinary options to keep their guests from spending on food and beverages somewhere outside. It's no longer surprising to see a bistro or a Starbucks within a hotel, with guests sipping a hot cup of coffee while having an official meeting or catching up with an old friend. If you're looking for entertainment options, these new spaces offer everything—from rooftop terraces with white couches and skyline vistas to musical performances by renowned artists.

A Change in the Scenario

It has been quite a while since the hotel industry realised the need to make lobbies a more accessible place for social interactions to take place, and this is precisely why most of the reputed hotel biggies have been going all out to include the best facilities for their customers. The Crystal City Marriott was one of the first conversions in this arena, ever since Marriott rolled out the 'Greatroom lobby' concept.

For instance, Schrager's 370-room Public Hotel on Manhattan's Lower East Side houses three bars, including a lobby hangout and nightspot with 360-degree views of the city. The guests also have an option to pick from two restaurants, of which the main one has sumptuous meals from a menu designed by Jean-Georges Vongerichten.

San Diego has many hotels that have embraced this change with vigour. The Embassy Suites San Diego Bay ditched the signature lagoons for a more modern atrium and casual seating during their $8.5 million renovation. Humphrey's Half Moon Inn and Suites replaced their '60s look with a contemporary setting that encompasses an all-stucco exterior accented with columns clad in stone. Hotel Palomar converted 20 unsold condos and two penthouse units on its upper floors into a collection of 50 rooms.

The techniques previously used by frat houses, wine bars, and art museums are now being increasingly used by hotels to transform their lobbies into spaces where both guests as well as non-guests can hang out. This has proven to be very effective in promoting their brand name. Lionel Ohayon, founder and CEO of ICRAVE, says, "Most people live an enormous digital life. People need to be reintroduced to being in public." And this is exactly what hotels are doing in making lobbies hip and happening hangout areas for their guests.

Big Data and Analytics: What Role Do They Play in the Hospitality Sector?

Big data sounds like a technical term that is best left to technical experts for technical purposes. But surprisingly, it has applications across different industries, even the one that thrives solely on human interaction and satisfaction, like hospitality.

Big data and data analytics are taking the world by storm, and it's not the IT sector alone that's embracing the data culture. Owing to its varied applications, big data analytics is making its presence felt in different industries, including travel and hospitality. But before you can leverage big data to increase your check-ins, let me familiarise you with the concept of big data.

In layman's language, big data refers to large sets of data, both structured and unstructured. The information that comes in can be extremely varied and from all kinds of sources. But it's not the volume of the data sets that makes big data valuable, it's what you can do with it that makes it almost indispensable to businesses.

In the hospitality industry, the data procured by hotels can be used to gain insights that can lead to strategic business decisions. By analysing the big data, you can predict customer behaviour patterns, enhance service offerings by offering personalised experiences, streamline the operations of your establishment, and recognise problem areas, if any.

Let's look at some of the specific use cases of big data within the hospitality industry.

Revenue Management

Big data can help hotels construct a foolproof revenue management strategy. By combining the data collected within the hotel and data available online, hotels can carry out predictive analyses, allowing hoteliers to anticipate the demand for hotel rooms accurately. Because even though hotel rooms are a fixed resource, the price for accommodation is elastic. It changes according to numerous factors like demand, weather, time of the year, etc.

Lavishly priced accommodations tend to lose revenue to their less pricey market rivals. And charging too little will either turn away customers due to suspicion or you'll be leaving money behind on the table. As a number of factors are to be considered while determining the cost of a room, it classifies as a data-intensive task. Data can be used to predict demand, including a few key metrics. These will include past occupancy rates and the number of rooms booked, along with external key metrics such as local events and school holidays. The more useful data points a hotel can get, the more capably it will be able to provide for future conditions, leading to better pricing decisions.

Once all the data is analysed, hotel owners can use big data to predict demand. They can then determine the right price to maximise profit and optimise the revenue generation process further.

Customer Categorisation and Targeted Marketing

No two travellers are the same. From travelling for business to travelling for pleasure to travelling on a budget to travelling luxuriously, hotel guests are incredibly varied in their choices. And big data provides hoteliers with the ability to identify the best opportunities for their hotel and target key demographics via online marketing. Hotels can then use both location and time-specific marketing to reach prospective customers at a time when advertising will be most relevant to them and on a platform where they are most likely to see it.

That includes everything ranging from understanding the customers' characteristics and behaviours to adjusting amenities to suit their requirements. You can differentiate between customers in different segments by analysing customer demographics. And this is imperative because while one customer might have a lavish spending budget for a single weekend, he/she might not be a frequent visitor. However, another traveller might not have a huge budget, but he might be a frequent visitor, and therefore, more profitable. In this way, big data can assist hoteliers in targeting their audience and divert their marketing efforts to the travellers they cater to.

Enhanced Customer Experience

To enhance customer experience, businesses must be able to gauge customer preferences. And the best way to do that is by collecting customer-specific data from different sources. Examining this data will provide the hotel with important insights into the customer's likes and dislikes. That is not all. Big data can also help hoteliers and customer service to spot patterns in customer opinions and get feedback regarding their strengths and weaknesses. It can also enhance customer experience according to the likes and dislikes of their guests.

Now, this may require collecting data sets that include service usage data, feedback from guests on social media platforms, reviews and testimonials posted on websites, and other similar information. And since hospitality is one sector where customers are more than happy to share their opinions, sorting through all this data and analysing it will be challenging. However, it is imperative as data analysis allows hotel owners to understand customers' preferences.

So you see, big data not only improves the customer experience but also promotes customer loyalty. Consequently, your hotel will not only gain incremental revenue but will also be rewarded with customer loyalty.

Identifying Issues within the Hotel

Every hotel has a few flaws, but ignoring them will lead to loss of money and give your hotel a bad name. Therefore, identifying these problems and their root cause is crucial. This is where big data comes in. It helps you find the discrepancies occurring in the hotel, allowing you to take the necessary measures to prevent them in the future.

For instance, if you take a look at the hotel's daily workings' report and spot that a particular item has been ordered in excess and wasted several times, you can hold the hotel staff responsible. Without the assistance of big data, you might have missed out on this type of information amidst the hustle and bustle of running a hotel.

That's not all. The collected data can be further used to discover flaws in house operations, measure productivity, manage resources effectively, and more. So, accumulation and analysis of the data are advantageous for the careful identification of issues in a hotel.

The Takeaway

The hospitality sector is still wrapping its head around the concept of big data, but they're waking up to the numerous ways it can help hotels generate more revenue and deliver a better experience. Besides, the amount of data originating from historical records, point-of-sale devices, current consumer habits, customer feedback, referrals, and online reviews is vast. With so much information pouring in from all directions, it would be a shame to let it all go to waste.

Moreover, big data and analytics have the potential to transform the hospitality industry and revolutionise the customer experience. As a result, the hospitality sector is already making huge strides towards a full-on embrace of big data and all the benefits it has to offer. In fact, a few industry bigwigs have already begun adopting long-term strategies and policies for big data management.

With so many companies embracing the big data trend and applying it to enhance their revenue, and customer service, big data seems to be crucial for maintaining a competitive edge in the future.

"Be so good they can't ignore you."

— Steve Martin

Never Have Empty Rooms Again: Essential Sales Strategies Every Hotel Can Use

The competitive nature of the hospitality industry is a given. And when it comes to securing guest reservations, the competition gets even tougher. Therefore, every hotelier needs to have an effective sales strategy that will bring in bookings every single time.

A thriving business depends on the occupancy of your rooms. After all, nobody becomes a hotelier to walk down a hallway of empty rooms. But that ill fate could be lurking around the corner, just a few wrong decisions away.

If you don't want to explore the bad side of your luck, you need to design sales strategies that will continually bring in more guests throughout all seasons. Of course, no one thing works for all. Every hotel has its unique selling points, target audience, and drawbacks. They will need to implement a sales strategy that is customised to their requirements and see what works best for their own target audience as well as for their local destination. But before you get started, below are some of the top hotel room sales strategies you should consider.

Direct Booking Sales Strategy

A hotel reservation system that facilitates direct online booking through your website has more than one benefit. With agents and distribution partners out of the scene, there's no commission to pay to third parties. This means more revenue generation for your hotel. Direct bookings also allow you to collect data that can guide the formation of marketing campaigns to attract guests.

Allowing your visitors to book their preferred rooms will also positively impact the guest experience. And don't forget to sync your hotel's reservation system with social media platforms. This allows guests to view pictures of your property, check for guest reviews, and make enquiries before making reservations by simply clicking on the link provided with the picture.

Cross-Promotional Sales Strategy

Having a great sales strategy during the holiday season or the peak months of the year is excellent; however, that alone isn't going to cut it. If you want to improve your hotel's occupancy at all times, you should also pay attention to what's going on in your city.

From industry conferences to concerts, festivals, sports events and more, always stay au courant on the events taking place in your city, especially in and around your area. Huge events always mean an influx of travellers, and that means people looking for accommodation. So, the next step is to plan a sales strategy with exciting promotions that will lure them to you. Create tie-up packages and launch campaigns to create themes based on those events or offer services or merchandise to match the occasion. It's the perfect opportunity for your hotel to welcome and wow the guests who booked with you.

Guest Rewards Sales Strategy

Who doesn't love gifts? Your guests definitely do. So, put a system in place that recognises and rewards guests for staying frequently or for purchasing upgrades. With more benefits and privileges, they will always come back to you. And if you want to increase your reservations through them, you should implement a reward system for referrals. That way, not only will you get more customers, but your current guests will act as ambassadors for your brand. And if you're able to live up to the reputation they've built up for you, it will turn into a never-ending loop of referrals, rewards, and bookings. This strategy is arguably the best if you want to generate repeat bookings.

Destination Marketing Sales Strategy

Destination marketing is huge these days. From destination weddings to destination birthday bashes—it's a massive trend that's showing no signs of going away anytime soon. Destination marketing campaigns drive more traffic to the area, and as a result, to the hotel. So, tap into a vast possibility of revenue generation. Collaborate with tourism business professionals to promote the region as a whole. From nature to architecture to history, you can lure in guests with a variety of USPs. Food destinations is a growing trend as well. So, you can plan campaigns around local wine tasting, local farmers' markets, street food and more to lure in food enthusiasts.

Revenue Management Sales Strategy

Seasons come and go, and with it, the guests do, too. So, what can you do to ensure that your hotel is always bustling with guests? Turn to the oldest trick in the travel and hospitality book— manage the price of the rooms according to the season. Low seasons usually mean slow business so, to encourage bookings and increase reservations, you should drop room rates. There's a whole group of tourists who travel to certain places during off-seasons due to low expenses. So, offering them a decent rate is a no-brainer if you want an immediate booking. In the same way, raise prices during high traffic times because guests are going to be willing to pay more to get a room.

As a hotel operator, you should strive to provide your guests with a comfortable and memorable stay. It is one of your most important responsibilities. But you should also remember that you are running a business. And for your business to be successful, you will need to sell rooms. The key is to balance both guest experience and business revenue while ensuring that you don't drive customers away with relentless in-your-face sales strategies. It's not easy, but as long as you keep values like authenticity at the heart of your operations and add a human touch to your communication, you will do just fine.

Sustainable Tech for Sustainable Tourism: Are You on the Uptake Yet?

At one time, sustainable luxury was considered a niche segment but recent changes in the sensibilities of travellers have forced the hospitality industry to make green travel less of a niche and more of a necessity. And aiding hotels in this quest is a slew of sustainable technologies.

When you think of sustainable hospitality, your mind immediately pans to a hotel set amidst manicured gardens with guests sipping tea with a bluebird perched on their shoulder singing melodiously to them. Okay, that bluebird bit might have been a bit too far-fetched, but you get the general idea of what I am trying to say here. These days, however, hotels have to do a lot more than scout for a location right in the middle of a verdant orchard to qualify for the sustainable tag. Something like this might have worked in the '80s but modern tourists are in search of genuinely eco-friendly and responsible organisations. The millennials now demand experiences that are as luxurious as they can be but with a healthy dose of sustainability thrown in for good measure.

And there's only one thing that can bring the two together—technology.

As you can see, sustainable tourism is no longer a niche or a trend; it is the future of travel. So, if you are a hotelier looking to get into the sustainable hospitality game, now's the time to start. Here are a few ways by which tech-driven sustainability practices can help you adopt the eco-friendly route and give your hotel a significant boost in the eyes of the planet-friendly crowd.

Reducing and Tracking Wastage

Go paperless, go digital: Digitising your communication and booking process can make a huge difference. Currently, your staff might be using paper for every little deed. But it doesn't have to be that way. Curb the use of paper by replacing paper receipts with email receipts for customers. You can also digitise your feedback forms, billing, and online record registers. All this, combined with an online audit trail, can reduce the use of paper drastically.

Sustainable laundry is the way to go: It has been estimated that laundry services contribute roughly 15–20% of a hotel's carbon footprint. Asking your guests to reuse their towels is one way to cut down on energy and water consumption. However, if you combine these efforts with sustainable laundry technology, you can certainly diminish your footprint. For example, a self-cleaning linen tech will significantly reduce your energy consumption and water consumption and reduce the frequency with which clients ask for bedding changes.

Automatic light switches to curb electricity wastage: Eco-friendly hotels track their energy consumption and strive to save energy by using energy-efficient technologies. In most hotels, the lights are often left on throughout the facilities even if they're not being used. Sometimes, even guests leave the lights on when they check out. So, investing in technologies such as occupancy sensors and LED lighting can do wonders to reduce energy waste. Such efforts will not only be cost-effective but will also earn you brownie points in the eyes of an eco-conscious traveller.

Eco-Friendly Power and Transportation

Alternate power generation source: Between running a hotel, offering luxurious amenities to your guests, and keeping commercial appliances continually running, your hotel's carbon footprint goes off the charts. Besides, energy is expensive, so why not look for alternative energy sources? Think natural energy generation sources like solar energy. Besides, your roof is already getting baked by the sun, so why not use it to your advantage? Additionally, it is the perfect spot to install solar panels without compromising on aesthetics.

Green fitness: Just like the hotel's kitchen or laundry room, the gym is also a huge source of carbon emissions. Regular workout equipment uses a lot of electricity. It's time to swap them with sustainable gym equipment. Sustainable workout equipment will not only reduce energy but will actually produce it. Once the equipment is plugged in and a user starts using it, the machine will harness the energy generated by the user. The machines also show the amount of electricity generated by users, which can act as an incentive for them to keep going.

Promoting Sustainable Tourism

Hybrid and electric vehicles for local transportation: If your hotel offers transportation to your guests, using hybrid or electric vehicles for the same will go a long way to show your customers that you're willing to do your bit for the environment. The maintenance cost of hybrid buses is quite low as they require less maintenance as compared to their diesel-run counterparts and offer fuel efficiency. You can even curate a few activities like outings to local parks, a tour of the major tourist attractions, a visit to museums, etc.

Virtual tours: This is something that will fascinate sustainable travellers who are worried about disturbing natural habitats. You could offer virtual tours for visitors who are curious about places of cultural significance. Creating virtual tours can take them on an educational journey, satisfying their curiosity about the local wildlife and tourist spots. To up the experience, you can also record audio and video stories from local community leaders, guides, and residents to make for an authentic and immersive experience.

Sustainable luxury was long regarded as an oxymoron until the recent changes in the hospitality industry made green travel less of a niche and more of a necessity. Now, the world is your sustainably farmed oyster. Moreover, implementing this sustainable tech will not only help your hotel attract a whole demographic of eco-travellers but will also minimise your hotel's environmental impact. To ensure that this demographic is reached, it is essential that hotels validate their green accomplishments. Beyond obtaining new customers, such initiatives will also educate your existing clientele by showing them that luxurious hospitality and eco-consciousness can go hand-in-hand. This will not only retain them but will give them a better reason to stay loyal customers.

When you think of AI and its applications, your mind always runs to science and tech-based industries. Does it have a role to play in hospitality—a sector that's driven by human interaction? Surprisingly, yes!

Artificial intelligence, or AI, seems to be the catchall phrase for technology that simulates human intelligence. It is now ubiquitous in almost every industry, where it's improving efficiency in countless different ways. After digitising the entertainment and IT sector, AI has moved on to the hospitality sector, which is eager to roll out the welcome mat and change the way it operates.

In recent years, the hospitality sector has evolved at an astonishing pace to deliver the best possible experience for the new generation of digitally savvy guests. And AI fits perfectly into this new, reshaped landscape. Thanks to AI's ability to extract data about guests and turn it into actionable insights, hotels can now use this data to offer a customised experience that they can monetise.

Here are a few scenarios that demonstrate how AI is revolutionising the hospitality sector.

AI-Powered Check-Ins

The gruelling routine of having to wait in line at a hotel's registration desk to check in will soon become a thing of the past. In fact, several hotels are doing away with reception desks altogether. Instead, guests can now use AI-enabled check-ins to bypass formal registration and verification. Hoteliers are now appointing a personalised multilingual AI valet that uses facial recognition for verification and to stay updated about the guest's arrival. It also assigns a room based on the guest's preferences and sends an e-key for the room to their phones upon arrival.

Eliminating the conventional check-in process not only drives direct bookings but also promotes guest loyalty by orchestrating better online experiences. And let's not dismiss the reduced employee costs that establishments enjoy by automating the entire process. Furthermore, AI analyses the data generated during the booking process, identifies which variations yielded better results, and evolves accordingly. So, since it learns from every interaction, it continually improves the knowledge and service it imparts.

Proximity-Based Assistance

AI assistance has established itself in everyday functioning, giving global travellers a lot more power. It can serve as a tour guide, concierge, and personal assistant all rolled into one. Guests can use AI to book cabs, ask for restaurant suggestions, check out local sightseeing, order room service, and ask any hotel-related query. AI can help guests get answers to any travel-related question, no matter how specific they might be, and receive answers almost instantly.

Gone are the days when travellers had to rely on the likes of Siri, Echo, Alexa, etc., to get the information they needed. These voice-activated AI assistants make travelling much more relaxed and personable. And the result? Rave reviews that generate loyalty, lead to repeat clientele, rope in new customers, and thus, generate more revenue.

Wi-Fi That Doesn't Fail You

High-speed internet is no longer a luxury; it's a necessity that every traveller demands. One might even say that an excellent wireless network takes precedence over a luxurious, expansive property situated in a picturesque location. And more often than not, traditional wireless networks fail to provide an uninterrupted connection or reliable service in a large estate, leaving guests frustrated.

AI-powered wireless platforms can better read usage patterns and troubleshoot problems on their own to give guests a more consistent and dependable Wi-Fi experience. So, if the internet connection takes a dip, the AI assistant on the guest's phone will let them know the status of the problem and the estimated time for it to be fixed. AI-powered Wi-Fi will also keep a log of the data usage and inform the hotel staff if the usage is about to reach the maximum limit.

Premium Customer Service

The potential for AI to improve the service aspect of the hospitality sector is vast. Having realised this, hotels are focused on harnessing that potential to enhance customer experience and generate more revenue. AI dabbles in a lot of hospitality-related departments. Apart from replacing the front desk, it can also allow guests to place an order without any waiting time. In fact, AI bots are now capable of delivering food and beverages to the guest's door.

AI can also be of massive help in the cleaning and maintenance department. Thanks to their attention to detail and precision, AI will be extremely efficient in sticking to schedules. It will also maintain the highest standards of cleanliness when it comes to preparing for the guest's arrival.

Power Management with AI

There has been a sudden surge in sustainable hospitality, all thanks to the increase in the number of eco-friendly travellers. Moreover, careless use of lighting, air conditioning, and heating can eat into more than 10% of a hotel's annual revenue. Sensors imbued with AI technology can sense the lights and appliances that are currently being used while turning off those that aren't to save power.

With AI, hotel staff can even monitor and manage guest data to intelligently turn the systems on and off to optimise guest comfort. Some hotels also provide guests with options to adjust the light intensity and temperature of the room so that they match their predetermined preferences.

AI-Recommended Travel Itinerary

Instead of turning to local tour guides to plan their travel schedules, tourists will always prefer AI-generated itineraries. This is because AI'' algorithm-based approach will sift through millions of travel preferences across various hospitality sectors that are stored in its database and combine them with the travellers' preferences. It will then put together a customised itinerary for each guest based on his or her preferences.

Apart from providing reliable and intuitive recommendations, AI's 24/7 service will ensure that guests always have an agent within reach in cases where flight delays or hotel snafus threaten a trip. Such upgrades in the hospitality sector will not only guarantee an increase in revenue but also add to the credibility of your hotel.

AI: The Future

The hospitality sector has experienced a massive disruption in the last few years. The influx of social media networks and other review sites has made it easier for customers to make their voices heard. This is forcing hotels to be more competitive than ever. And artificial intelligence, combined with machine and symbolic learning, has the power to drive a new frontier of futuristic opportunities. It can tailor experiences to customers' preferences, manage day-to-day tasks, streamline the hotel's process, and more. And this is what allows hotels to carve out a competitive edge and not only survive but also thrive in the ever-evolving hospitality sector.

Great companies are built by people who never stop
thinking about ways to improve the business.

– J. Willard "Bill" Marriott

Hospitality Industry, After the Millennials, Are You Ready for Gen Z?

Dear hoteliers, Gen Z is going to be knocking on your doors very soon. Are you ready to meet them? Often described as millennials on steroids, Gen Z is far more demanding than millennials. How will you win their approval? What do you need to do to get in their good books?

Across different industries, marketing strategies are increasingly shifting from generic to more targeted. From geo-specific audiences to even subsets of a broader demographic, marketers are trying everything. The next big set that's in focus is 'Generation Z' or 'iGeneration'. And the hospitality industry is no exception.

Generation Z, or Gen Z as they are called, comprises young but more influential minds. This generation is not just tech-savvy, but they have the power to drive the crowd in any direction with a stronger online presence than any other generation ever!

Already being referred to as 'millennials on steroids', Gen Z is the new cultural wave in town. While millennials were young adolescents in the year 2000, Gen Z was just born. This means the oldest of Gen Z would currently be about 18 years of age and stepping into adulthood. Their perception of human interactions is very different, and several instances indicate that Gen Z is more forward-thinking, progressive, and adaptive than any other generation in the past. Most importantly, they are self-aware, mature, and have more clarity in their thoughts and decisions. So, if hoteliers thought their work of adapting to a new generation had come to an end with millennials, they should brace themselves because Gen Z is going to be knocking on their doors very soon.

How is Gen Z Affecting the Hospitality Industry?

Consider the following findings:

84% of seven to 17-year-olds hold a strong influence on the family's overall expenditure

Long gone are the days when parents didn't need their children's inputs on household expenses and other decisions. Today, Gen Z holds the reins to the virtual world in most families, allowing them to have a better understanding of the choices of every member of the family, including what to buy, where they should dine, which part of the world they should travel to for holidays, or where they can stay while on vacation.

While 32% of parents admit that their kids hold a lot of influence on vacations and their budget, 54% of parents say kids have some influence.

The rules of the game are changing rapidly, and the hospitality industry's marketing strategy needs to keep pace with it. While business hotels are targeting millennials, leisure hotels should actively start targeting Gen Z.

The young millennials are not to be sidelined, of course. Overall, the 22 to 31-year-old millennial travellers are worth around $200 billion. However, the Digital Tourism Think Tank (DTTT) points out that Gen Z currently forms one-fourth of the population, and by 2020, will account for 40% of all consumers. This is a clear indicator that they cannot be ignored.

How Do You Attract Gen Z to Your Hotel?

While what attracts Gen Z is not very different from millennials, their approach towards them is. Let's look at a few examples

Online presence: Gen Z is digitally well-connected. In fact, 92% of Gen Z has a digital footprint, out of which 25% are more likely than millennials to say that they are addicted to their digital devices. This means hoteliers need to have a solid digital presence to be discovered by them.

And how do you go about doing that? Be present where they are—on social media. You must get active online and promote your property and amenities wherever Gen Z hangs out. Stay in touch with what's 'trending' and what Gen Z is up to in the digital world so you can jump into the conversations there as well.

Community experience: The days of 'I want to be alone' are long gone. Gen Z is noticeably focused on aligning with community culture. They value experiences over material possessions, and the ability to meet and mingle with others is an integral part of travel. They want to make friends along the way and prefer a more 'connected' experience rather than just going to a place, checking out its attractions, and returning home. Hotels that offer communal seating, social hubs, and dining and common areas for guests wishing to interact with others are more likely to catch Gen Z's attention.

Commitment and Loyalty

Gen Z has a more elevated perception of loyalty. They are as loyal to brands as brands are loyal to them. If you're able to honour your commitments, you'll earn their trust, and if you exceed their expectations, they're likely to become your lifelong fans. But disappoint them, and they will not spare you. As fair as they are with their compliments, they are straightforward with their criticism. While millennials were more forgiving and adjusting, Gen Z is not. So, make sure you keep up your side of the commitment before you expect them to be loyal customers. And should you earn their approval, they'll be more than happy to act as promoters of your brand on social media.

What Will Hotels Get from All This?

Apart from a base of new customers and dedicated brand advocates, hotels will be able to raise user-generated content that will leave a global impression about them without much ado.

Gen Z is very comfortable with crowdsourcing information about future purchases like travel, destinations, hotels, restaurants, etc. They base their decisions to put money on reviews by strangers, friends, and influencers and believe they have a duty to contribute to the conversation. In the digital world, it's called engagement. And Gen Z isn't afraid to engage. So, your job is to keep them happy. A happy Gen Z customer means more and more engagement and impressions on your profiles. However, a goof-up from your end can result in a massive backlash, which can damage your reputation and revenue.

The bottom line is this: Generation Z is on its way. And hotel brands wanting to remain relevant and competitive in the future have limited time to prepare for this audience. In this changing scenario, without ample support from digital technology to run your day-to-day operations, you simply cannot focus on the 'what's next'. If you want to be a long-term player in the hospitality industry, it's about time you get a dynamic system in place that will help you strategise and brainstorm for the future.

Wellness-Themed or Authentic Wellness Hotels? What Have You Got to Offer?

In the pursuit of maintaining or enhancing one's well-being, travellers are looking for wellness tourism. For these health-conscious travellers, wellness is no longer about going to a fitness centre but rather about the impact the experience at the property has on the guest's physical, mental, and psychological well-being—during and after the stay. And while the demand for health and wellness facilities is known to the hospitality industry, there are two types of such facilities that hoteliers can invest in—wellness-themed hotels and authentic wellness retreats.

As wellness and fitness go from luxury to necessity, the hospitality industry worldwide is finding innovative ways to implement the concept in every aspect of their customer's experience. From the basic layout of the property to daily operations, hoteliers are no longer restricting their services to an exclusive spa session or swimming pool on the premises.

In a 2017 report, the Global Wellness Institute (GWI) estimated that wellness travel was a $639.4 billion market in 2017, growing more than twice as fast as the regular travel industry. This was all thanks to health-conscious travellers who spent as much as 130% more on hotel amenities than other guests. The same report also projected that wellness tourism would continue to flourish as the majority of travellers considered wellness and fitness facilities on a property as a key deciding factor. GWI also predicted that global wellness tourism would reach $919 billion by 2022, representing 18% of the global tourism market.

But who are these wellness-seeking tourists? What are they looking for in a hotel? Wellness tourism targets two types of travellers: primary and secondary wellness travellers.

- **Primary wellness travellers**: These are travellers who take a trip or choose a destination depending on its health and wellness offerings. In other words, their primary purpose of travel is wellness. These travellers visit wellness retreats bi-yearly or even quarterly. They participate in yoga, meditation, detox, and other traditional wellness regimes.

- **Secondary wellness travellers**: These are people who are health-conscious even on the go. They strictly follow a diet, and their fitness routine in the gym is the highlight of their day. They regularly indulge in detox products and massage sessions. These travellers accounted for 86% of wellness expenditure in 2017 according to the GWI report.

Now that we know wellness travellers and their mindset and preferences, let us talk about what the hospitality industry has to offer them.

As the wellness and hospitality industries are gradually interweaving, Horwath HTL presented an industry report comparing two variations of the health and wellness hospitality industry, namely, wellness-themed hotels and wellness hospitality.

While wellness-themed hotels provide everything a health-conscious traveller can dream of, an authentic wellness development space is not just a place to relax and shed a few kilos. It is a retreat to make health and fitness changes that last beyond the vacation.

In-room features: A typical wellness-themed in-room service often includes a workout station with the latest fitness equipment and mobile applications to guide travellers on their fitness regime through their stay. These rooms also have minibars well stacked with protein shakes, nutritious bars, and other supplements, taking care of all the needs of a secondary traveller.

On the other hand, the in-room service of an authentic wellness development includes a self-indulging yoga or meditation corner where travellers can relax and unwind. These rooms are set to offer various extensions of the healing process. In the bathrooms, you can find a vitamin C shower that nourishes your hair and skin and eliminates the harmful cocktail of chemicals like chlorine and ammonia present in city water. In rooms, there is a supply of ozone-enriched air so that you can breathe in the freshness of the mountain air. These rooms often don't have any devices that cause distraction from the purpose of the visit. Hence no TV, mobile phone, or even minibar inside the room.

On-premise facilities: While a wellness-themed hotel allows its health-conscious guests to pick from a menu of wholesome food and beverages, an authentic wellness hotel provides a customised diet plan. These wellness retreats not only equip their guests with diet and health consultations during the stay but offer pre- and post-consultation as well.

A highly reputed wellness-themed hotel often has various fitness programs and services to offer, from running and cycling club memberships to swimming pools, sauna baths, and massage sessions. A true wellness establishment, however, offers facilities that customers may not find in regular life—uniquely customised workout sessions like yoga, Zumba, or weight training. Here, a personal wellness concierge not only focuses on a customer's physical but mental and emotional well-being as well.

These authentic wellness hotels enable a sense of community. In today's fast-paced lifestyle, we often tend to forget about the social community we live in. These wellness retreats help people remember the responsibilities they have towards the people around them. It also connects them with the beauty, sensibility, and sensitivity of nature.

Other property-related initiatives: While wellness-themed hotels collaborate with big health and fitness brands, authentic wellness hotels form an association with wellness experts and clinics. Sustainable initiatives, like organic gardening and the use of renewable energies, are an integral part of wellness-themed properties.

On the other hand, a true wellness hotel is established upon wellness community standards that cater to the overall well-being of a person. Most importantly, these wellness centres have a biophilic approach to building community within the premises. This biophilic architecture not only helps to reduce stress and anxiety and clean all negative thoughts but also improves cognitive skills and creativity and expedites healing.

Both the types of hotels that we've discussed above have the same aim of offering guests the benefits of health and wellness. However, their approaches towards it are entirely different. Today, wellness isn't just about health food or luxurious facilities. Wellness simply refers to creating an environment in which guests can relax and bond with others with a sense of being and spirit. Today's generation is aware of the value of wellness. The hospitality industry just has to make an effort and provide that touch of wellness to its guests.

Remember not only to say the right thing
in the right place, but far more difficult still,
to leave unsaid the wrong thing
at the tempting moment.

– Benjamin Franklin

It takes a lot to run a business successfully. But one aspect that hoteliers often ignore is communication, not just with guests but also inter-departmental. Having a strong communication strategy can be the key to customer satisfaction.

The hotel industry is always in flux, with different trends, updates in technology, and changes in consumer behaviour shaping and reshaping it time and again. But one thing that remains constant is the importance of customer satisfaction.

Customer satisfaction is the lifeline of a hotel, and they do everything they can to ensure that the guests have amazing and memorable experiences during their stay. But this isn't restricted to the services and amenities they provide or how beautiful the property and location are. Customer satisfaction is also tied to the interactions that consumers have with the business itself. Thus, creating a powerful and effective communication strategy is the key to success in the hospitality industry. Here are a few things that you can do when starting your communication strategy.

Be Regular

Regular communication helps you stay at the forefront of the consumer's long list of options. Periodic emails and messages with your latest offers, updates, or just friendly reminders to catch their attention can make a lot of difference in the customer's selection.

When sending out regular communication, make sure it's not your garden variety generic content. Each message should have something useful for your consumers—a coupon, an offer, an interesting achievement, or happy news. Bombarding them with only sales content will put them off for good.

Also, pace yourself well. You don't need to send an email or message every day. This can overwhelm them. Be regular, but don't turn into a bother. Flood their inbox, and you will be marked spam faster than you can say 'Offer'! Keep your communication steady, consistent, and considerate at all times.

Regular communication should also extend to interactions during their stay. Ensuring they have everything they need and asking for feedback about the various aspects of their stay is a good step towards creating a long-lasting relationship with guests, further bolstering brand loyalty.

Personalise Your Communication

The biggest problem companies face with their communication strategy is that it comes across as too impersonal, which discourages consumers from responding to them. And why would they? We all get dozens of emails and messages a day. How interested would we be in something that's flat and boring? Not a lot.

That's why it's important to never lose sight of what your customers like. Their preferences, interests, choice of cuisine at your restaurant, and even the time of the year they travel can be used to create engaging content. And helping you in this is customer relationship management (CRM).

CRM data can give you a detailed report about your consumers, which can help you plan your communication strategy. This not only helps the business increase its profitability by investing in key areas highlighted in the report but also helps attract positive customer responses.

Be Human

A good communication strategy places equal importance on what you say and how you say it. A message that is stripped of personality will never land. Hotels are a service-based industry; they keep the human element at the core of everything they do. Then why should the communication be robotic? Understand your target audience and make your messages relatable. Your audience is likely to read it without losing interest and connect with you better and forge a stronger relationship.

Why go through all this effort, you're wondering. Because it gives your business an authenticity that others lack. And if you're able to maintain that in online, offline, and in-person interactions, you're definitely doing the right thing.

Be Prompt

Customers often call or email the hotel asking them about their services directly. And their queries tend to slip through the cracks and go unattended. Or, if they are attended to, they don't receive the kind of attention they deserve. Understandably, customers become disgruntled and leave with a bad feeling, possibly in search of a different service provider.

Be prompt in addressing customer concerns, regardless of where they originate from. Have pop-up chat boxes on your website and establish a quick turnaround time for queries. When the audience notices that you're prioritising them and doing everything you can to resolve an issue, they will truly believe that you're taking a customer-first approach. This also drives sales as customers are more likely to choose a company that keeps their needs before everything else.

Keep It Seamless

As much as interacting with guests is important, it is also vital to establish clear lines of communication internally. Communicating with the staff with clear, precise instructions is important to operate fluidly and maintain a consistent experience for guests.

One effective way to do this is to leave it to technology. It can be as big as a building-wide PA system or as small as a messenger app like Slack. It works perfectly as long as the staff gets the message and understands the instructions. You can also invest in training employees so they work like a well-oiled machine and provide the best experience possible to guests.

A personalised communication strategy and smooth internal operations can help a hotel achieve its main goals—to scale up the business by maximising profit and creating a more pleasant stay for guests. And after devising a strategy of effective communication, both for external and internal purposes, comes the time for amendments. It's not a venture; the hotel has to go it alone. Customer and employee feedback is important, too, steering the hotel's plans in the right direction.

Resilience: A Quality That Pulled The Hospitality Industry Back to its Feet

Caught on the dark side of the pandemic, the hospitality industry went through such dire straits that its survival seemed to be at stake. But if there's one thing about the sector that one can vouch for, it is that the industry is resilient and innovative. How it outlived the Covid-era is nothing less than remarkable. Today, as the sector revives and finds its foot back in the game, let's look back at its fighting spirit with pride.

Hospitality was one of the most affected industries by Covid-19. It is now on the path to complete recovery, but it saw a menacing period that threatened the sector's very existence. In the wake of the pandemic, the hospitality industry went through rapid and massive losses. Occupancy rates dropped drastically. As survival instincts kicked in, an unprecedented turmoil was triggered. Many hotels operated on limited capacities, and many more shut their doors. Millions of hospitality employees faced layoffs and furloughs, and the few who were retained had to work twice as hard on substantially reduced salaries. Things were pretty grim, and looming uncertainties shook the industry to the core. But the resilient sector fought back, and oh, how they fought!

There when needed: The hospitality industry has never been one that loses hope. Instead, it gives, despite all adversities. Looking back, it was a great moment of pride to see hotels worldwide, big or small, open their doors to healthcare and essential workers fighting the pandemic. Some others took the onus of delivering safe food to the ones who put the well-being of others before their health, like health care and law enforcement personnel. The industry known to carry the mantle of 'at your service' became even more human. It put up a united front undeterred by the economic williwaw it was facing.

The immediately after: Implementing Covid-safety measures and maintaining high cleanliness and hygiene were the need of the hour, which hotels incorporated promptly. But that wasn't all. Sprouting out of the do-or-die scenario, a new phase of great imagination, innovation, and transformation arose. The times of despair presented hospitality with a moment of epiphany. An industry highly dependent on personal interaction now had to find newer ways of delivering services and experiences in an era where in-person interaction with guests had to be shrunk to a bare minimum. And they found not one but many different ways to do so!

Business couldn't be as usual: By the time travel restrictions were lifted, people's desire to move out of the bounds of their homes heightened. While there was willingness, health and safety concerns prevailed. The way people travelled had changed, and guest behaviour had evolved. Hoteliers had to maintain their distance but still create a sense of warmth and offer the comfort guests seek. There wasn't a second option for hotels other than transforming the entire ecosystem of delivering services and experiences.

It was crucial that hotels evaluated, reinvented, and repositioned their offerings in the new normal. These were times when the good old one-size-fits-all approach wouldn't do the trick. People were looking for more than just a comfortable room, a fantastic restaurant, or modern amenities in a hotel. They wanted a meaningful, mindful escape from their pandemic-induced afflictions. Guest experiences now had to be deeper, more intimate, and more personal. Hotels quickly understood the change in guest behaviour. They revamped themselves to help guests reconnect with themselves, create memories with their loved ones, and share a space that provided a respite from the chaotic world outside. Hoteliers not only introduced slow experiences and well-being vacations, but they also tailored them to the guests' needs.

The newest tech graduate: These were times when sales calls or personal demonstrations of changes and updates were out of the question. A digital era was rising, and hospitality was determined to make the most of it. Hoteliers implementing innovative tech solutions also had to convey that theirs was a safe space so guests felt comfortable enough to stay in their hotels. It wasn't just communications that went digital—contactless processes for check-ins, check-outs, and payments, and QR scanners for food ordering soon became standard norms. And the industry did not rest just there—it graduated to become a tech-enabled sector, initiating a number of futuristic technologies in the coming days. From automated processes to AI-enabled in-room services and smart amenities to service robots, the hotel tech grew multifold in a short span.

Understanding what people wanted from hotel experiences and thoughtfully blending it with new-age technology helped hospitality players build a strong foundation to sustain in an extremely volatile business environment. Balancing technology with the quintessential human touch that hospitality has always been known for, hoteliers reconnected with their consumers, warmed up their relationships, and eventually regained the guests' trust.

Diversification for sustenance: As the world eventually learnt to live with the dangers of Covid-19, talks of revenge travel and a post-pandemic boom made rounds across the globe. But a complete recovery from the blow seemed like a distant dream for hotels. At the time, hoteliers had to focus on creating business models that could generate enough revenue to sustain—keeping business up and running was more crucial. Catering to the more immediate needs of people seemed to be a business-efficient approach. Diversifying existing spaces and services was a necessity that hospitality couldn't look away from.

Because people were eager to step out of their homes, hoteliers conceptualised unique offerings. Impressive ideas like hybrid hospitality, work from hotel, and workcations emerged for working professionals. For those who wanted to take a long break, hoteliers put forward long-haul stay offers, staycation packages, and offbeat experiences away from the crowds. Hotels that did not have such provisions welcomed wedding bookings, provided in-home catering services, and offered takeaways and food deliveries to supplement revenue loss. Many hotels and restaurants adopted small menus and limited hours of service. These helped manage the staff shortage, reduce wastage, and optimise available resources.

Hospitality always springs back: The hospitality industry is one of the most vulnerable to headwinds—economic or otherwise. Every time there is a change in global or local environments, hospitality is perhaps the first to be affected and one of the last to recover from slowdowns. But the fact that people remain curious to explore new places, discover new experiences, and learn along the way keeps the industry going.

Sooner or later, the stout industry manages to pull through in adverse times and spring back stronger and sharper. The Covid-19 era is no different. While bearing the brunt of the pandemic was one of the hardest things the industry had thus far gone through, hoteliers weathered the storm without losing the core values of service and hospitality. It quickly moved from being reactive to becoming immensely proactive. The industry demonstrated great resilience, something it must always treasure.

Failing Hotels: Competition Isn't the Only Factor to Be Blamed

Would you be surprised if I told you that not all hotels are profitable? In fact, most of them are in a pretty precarious position financially. But that's no reason to give up just yet. It's possible to turn a failing hotel around by studying the performance of different divisions and understanding the factors that are costing you your profitability.

Everywhere you go, you see that a slew of hotels—decades old to just a few days new, high-end ones to tier-three ones, and absolutely mundane establishments to bizarre and unique ones. Given the sheer number of hotels, it's only natural that stiff competition will make survival difficult and that rankings will continuously shuffle. However, when a hotel tanks, cut-throat competition isn't the only reason behind it.

Many factors contribute to a hotel's downward spiral, if not complete demise. And competition is just one of them. As hoteliers, you need to go beyond external factors and take everything into perspective so that you're able to devise a strategy that brings your dying establishment back to life, bubbling with activities and guests galore. And for that, here are the mistakes that you should avoid making.

Trends as Old as Days

The mistake: Not being updated with the industry trends is one of the most damaging things you can do to your business. If you first opened the doors of your hotel to guests 15 years ago, you can't lure present travellers with trends that are decades old.

The remedy: Keep pace with the trends and adapt to the changes. It isn't difficult to see that travellers then and now are very different. Staying in a hotel is no longer just about having a decent room with a well-made bed. Millennial guests expect experiences, and hotels are no exception. And outdated trends and technology become huge roadblocks to giving your guests what they desire.

Get on the eco-friendly wagon to appeal to the earth-loving travellers, get more updated technology to reduce wait time and increase efficiency, and mix the local and the global in your menu. In short, provide services that are meaningful and relevant to current travellers, and you should be just fine.

Weak USP and even Weaker Marketing

The mistake: Hotels need a strong selling proposition that will grab your customer's attention. But in addition, it's crucial to have an online presence. Considering that millennials and Gen Zs make up the highest percentage of travellers, and a staggering 97% of them are online, not having a digital marketing strategy in place could really hurt your hotel.

The remedy: First off, focus on your USP. Whether it's a scenic or prime location, good architecture, eco-friendly practices, or a mixture of all these, make it attractive. And try to keep it as unique as you can. If you're trying to market one feature of your hotel, stick to that feature and give your guests what they expect.

Once you have that figured out, work on building a brand presence on digital platforms. There's a host of platforms, and you can choose the ones that suit your property the best. Once you have an official account, post pictures of your property, interact with your followers, ask your guests to share their pictures and tag you—it's all a part of marketing while building a name and a reputation for your brand. Make sure you also have a neat, beautiful, and easy-to-navigate website. Fill your online gallery with attractive pictures of your property, collect and put up guest reviews and testimonials, and give visitors great deals and offers when they book a room.

Staff that Never Smiles

The mistake: The way your staff behaves plays a huge role in making guests feel welcome and comfortable. So, ensure your own staff is well-trained and motivated. Lack of regular training, poor working conditions, and zero incentives can reflect in your staff's demeanour and affect the way they handle your guests and resolve their queries and issues. Unhappy and untrained staff can potentially drag your hotel down and significantly hamper your reputation.

The remedy: It is vital that you keep your staff not just ready for every challenge and surprise this job brings but also happy. Apart from regular training on client handling, customer service, time management, housekeeping, etc., to improve their skills, you should award them with incentives and appreciative tokens. You should also work on staff and department coordination and their bond with each other. And for that, you can have team-building outings and activities.

Doing so will establish an environment of unity in the teams. They'll also be encouraged to engage in healthy competition, where they are continuously trying to improve themselves. And when you achieve this attitude in the staff, consider half the battle won. Therefore, it is of utmost importance that you have someone with excellent management skills handling the teams.

There's Always Extra Expenditure

The mistake: All hoteliers are aware of certain universal hotel expenditures that include fixed as well as variable costs. The fixed costs won't be affected by the hotel occupancy volume, and most of them are expenditures that you can't avoid. However, you can reduce or completely cut down on some costs. Food wastage, electricity consumption, outdated equipment... all of these add up to unnecessary expenses. But there are more unchecked areas that eat into your revenue which, in a matter of time, can bleed the financial health of your hotel dry.

The remedy: A healthy cash flow means a successful hotel. So, if your profit margin does not look favourable, check all the expenditures. In some instances, initial investments in cost-saving items like energy-conserving equipment will save you a lot in the long term. Many hotels also spend on advertising and sales and marketing. While these are unavoidable costs, you can definitely reduce the amount you're spending on them. Depending on what suits your hotel better, you can either have an in-house team or a contractual relationship with advertising and marketing agencies. You can also reduce the number of subscriptions, including newspapers and magazines.

Starting a hotel, while not exactly a walk in the park, is surprisingly not the most difficult part of the game. What's challenging is ensuring continuous smooth operations and keeping cash flow on the positive side. So, stay updated and aware of what's going on in the industry and inside your hotel. That will ultimately help you understand what you need to do to maintain your brand and keep it profitable.

Adapt, Survive, Thrive: The Hospitality Industry Writes a Story of Hope and Resilience in a Post-Pandemic World

The hospitality industry has shown great resilience and adaptability in the face of the Covid-19 pandemic. Initially hit hard by travel restrictions and plummeting occupancy rates, hotels had to employ creative strategies to survive. They adapted to changes in customer expectations by offering unique staycation experiences and prioritising wellness. Technological interventions like contactless check-in and enhanced cleanliness measures were implemented to ensure safety. Hotels also focused on sustainable practices, including energy and water conservation, waste reduction, and recycling. Through these efforts, the hospitality industry has emerged stronger and better equipped for the future.

The past three years have been a period of upheaval and transformation for the hospitality industry. As the world grappled with the sudden onslaught of the coronavirus, hotels and resorts found themselves at the storm's epicentre. The early days of the pandemic were marked by uncertainty and unprecedented hardship. Travel restrictions, border closures, and fear of contagion led to a dramatic decline in bookings and occupancy rates. Overnight, hotels that were once bustling with life became ghostly, with empty corridors and silent lobbies.

The losses incurred by hotels and all stakeholders were staggering and were a harsh wake-up call to the magnitude of the crisis. Global hotel occupancy rates plummeted to an all-time low of around 20% in April 2020, resulting in billions of dollars in revenue losses for the industry. Countless hotels were forced to shutter their doors temporarily or, in some unfortunate cases, permanently.

The impact rippled through the entire ecosystem, affecting employees, suppliers, and local economies that relied heavily on tourism. Hotels had to resort to drastic measures to stay afloat, laying off large numbers of employees, giving away room bookings at massive discounts, and (in some cases) offering up vacant rooms to medical facilities.

Hotels had to resort to creative thinking and explore alternative sources of income. Some properties collaborated with local businesses, offering space for conferences, workshops, and community events. Others ventured into online platforms, hosting virtual events and leveraging their expertise to provide personalised consulting services. Hoteliers capitalised on the emerging trend of remote work by creating attractive workcation packages. These offerings allowed guests to enjoy the hotel's amenities while balancing work responsibilities, catering to a new demographic of digital nomads and remote workers seeking inspiring environments.

But the losses weren't only financial in nature. The emotional toll on hoteliers, employees, and guests was palpable. The once-vibrant atmosphere of hotels, characterised by warmth, conviviality, and shared experiences, gave way to a sense of uncertainty and anxiety. The hospitality industry, known for its resilience, was confronted with an unprecedented challenge that demanded not only business acumen but also empathy to overcome it.

However, it was in the face of adversity that the true spirit of the hospitality industry emerged. In the midst of darkness, hotels began charting a path towards recovery, employing innovative strategies and embracing change to navigate the storm. It soon became evident that the hospitality industry's ability to adapt, innovate, and cater to evolving customer preferences would help it survive and emerge stronger than ever.

Let's reflect on the resilience and adaptability of the hospitality industry and see how they were able to triumph over Covid-19 challenges.

Understanding and Adapting to Changes in Customer Expectations

When the world finally started to reopen in 2022, hoteliers were met with a surprising reality: travel did not instantly rebound as expected. People had endured significant hardships and emerged with altered perspectives. The hospitality industry quickly recognised the need to address these changes and create new experiences for travellers.

One notable shift that emerged was the rise of staycations. People sought local getaways and looked for solace in familiar surroundings. Hotels responded by curating unique offerings that transformed traditional stays into memorable experiences. They provided a respite from daily routines, offering wellness retreats, spa treatments, and recreational activities to enhance the overall staycation experience.

Moreover, a greater emphasis on well-being emerged as travellers sought to rejuvenate their minds and bodies. Hotels invested in wellness facilities, expanded fitness centres, and introduced programs focused on mental health, such as yoga and meditation classes. These changes catered to evolving customer preferences and positioned hotels as holistic retreats for rejuvenation and self-care.

Implementing Technological Interventions for Human Comfort

Social distancing became necessary during the pandemic, compelling the hospitality industry to re-evaluate its operations and redefine customer touchpoints. In a bid to minimise physical contact and enhance safety, hotels swiftly adopted technological solutions.

One area that underwent significant transformation was communal-style restaurants and buffet services. Recognising the risk of shared serving utensils and self-serve stations, hotels shifted towards sit-down restaurants with spaced seating arrangements. These redesigned spaces incorporated features like QR code-based menus and antimicrobial surfaces, minimising touchpoints and reducing the potential for viral transmission. Some hotels also introduced grab-and-go food stations or equipped rooms with small kitchens, allowing guests to dine without leaving the property.

Another technology-driven change that gained momentum during the pandemic was contactless check-in. The industry witnessed a rapid shift towards app-based check-ins and digital keys, eliminating the need for in-person interactions and minimising contact with hotel staff. In-room amenities were also reimagined, with touchless controls for lighting, temperature, and entertainment systems.

Established hotel chains had already pioneered the use of digital keys, and they continued to enhance the app-based experience by integrating multiple hotel-stay functions. However, smaller hotel chains had to ensure that their applications offered substantial value to guests who were hesitant to download a hotel-specific app for a short stay.

Stronger Emphasis on Cleanliness and Sanitisation

Technology also played a crucial role in establishing and maintaining cleanliness standards. Hotels recognised the importance of formalising their 'clean initiatives' and sought certifications from third-party regulators/entities. They hired cleanliness managers, who developed comprehensive plans and trained employees on proper cleaning procedures, adhering to guidelines from health authorities. These measures included enhanced cleaning frequency, revised floor plans to promote social distancing, the installation of physical barriers, and the use of technologies like ultraviolet light to augment cleaning efforts. By implementing robust cleaning protocols and promoting their commitment to safety, hotels aimed to regain the public's trust and provide reassurance to guests.

Integrating technology into various aspects of the hospitality industry ensured the safety and well-being of guests and contributed to a seamless and efficient experience. By embracing contactless technologies, hotels were able to adapt to the changing landscape, meet customer expectations, and navigate the challenges posed by the pandemic.

Reimagining Operations to Implement Sustainable and Eco-Friendly Measures

The Covid-19 pandemic brought about a shift in travellers' mindsets, with an increasing emphasis on sustainable and eco-friendly choices. As individuals became more conscious of their lifestyle choices and carbon footprints, the hospitality industry recognised the need to align with these values and implement sustainable practices.

One of the key areas where hotels focused their efforts was energy conservation. Properties introduced energy-efficient systems and technologies to minimise energy consumption. Smart thermostats were installed to regulate room temperatures more efficiently, ensuring optimal comfort while reducing energy waste. LED lighting replaced traditional incandescent bulbs, offering energy savings and longer lifespans while reducing maintenance requirements. These energy-efficient measures not only contributed to cost savings for the hotels but also positively impacted the environment by reducing greenhouse gas emissions.

Water conservation was another crucial aspect of sustainable practices within the hospitality industry. Hotels implemented advanced plumbing technologies, such as low-flow showerheads and faucets, to reduce water consumption without compromising on the guest experience. Water recycling systems were also introduced, allowing hotels to reuse water for non-potable purposes such as irrigation and cleaning. By prioritising water conservation, hotels played a significant role in preserving this precious resource and promoting responsible water management.

Waste reduction and recycling programs were implemented to minimise the environmental impact of hotel operations. Hotels strongly emphasised reducing single-use plastics, such as disposable cutlery, straws, and toiletry containers. Many properties switched to eco-friendly alternatives made from biodegradable or compostable materials. Recycling stations were strategically placed throughout the premises to encourage guests and staff to segregate recyclable materials properly. Additionally, hotels embraced innovative approaches to repurpose and upcycle materials, transforming waste into valuable resources. For example, discarded furniture could be refurbished and used in other areas of the hotel or donated to local charities.

Furthermore, hotels made efforts to raise awareness among guests about their sustainable initiatives. By providing information in guest rooms, lobbies, and digital platforms, hotels educated travellers about the importance of sustainability and encouraged them to participate in eco-friendly practices during their stay. Some hotels even organised sustainability-themed activities and events, engaging guests and creating a sense of shared responsibility for the environment.

The Bright Future Ahead

Despite the immense challenges faced by the hospitality industry, its unwavering resilience and adaptability have positioned it for a bright future. As travel gradually rebounds, hotels that have embraced change are at the forefront of recovery. By staying attuned to evolving customer expectations, prioritising well-being, adopting sustainable practices, and diversifying revenue streams, hotels have not only weathered the storm but also set themselves apart as pioneers in the post-pandemic world. Their strength, determination, and ingenuity were bolstered by their ability to adapt and transform in the face of adversity. This was a testament to their unwavering commitment to customer satisfaction. With hope in our hearts, we look forward to a future where hotels continue to provide exceptional experiences, setting new benchmarks and forever cherishing the lessons learned during these extraordinary times.

FROM OUR
GUEST AUTHORS

**In the following section I have added
three chapters contributed by guest authors.**

Shooting a Movie in your Hotel: A Buzz Builder or a Buzz Killer!

By Akhilesh Gupta

Shooting movies in your hotel—does it ultimately add value to your estate and increase the overall revenue/profitability in the long run? Or is it just a lot of hype, with short-term losses, caused due to the shutting down of your property for filming?

A young, strong, wise Robert De Niro, walking past the slot machines in *Casino*.

A SWAT team led by Brad Pitt marching out of the Bellagio in *Oceans 13*.

A shirtless David Hasselhoff with his army of blonde bombshells running out of the five-star resort in Waikiki to rescue a drowning guy in *Baywatch Hawaii*.

Roger Moore and Maud Adams walking around in the gardens of the Taj Lake Palace in the Bond movie *Octopussy*.

Watching these scenes always makes me wonder if such a strategy would help promote a hotel and make it visible to the masses. In the day and age of the internet and social media, hotels can boost their online presence using any number of tools and techniques. So is there merit in using old-fashioned strategies of letting film production companies use your hotel to shoot a scene?

We also have to consider the reward versus the cost of shutting down your business for a couple of days so that a few movie scenes could be shot on your premises. We must understand that some of these properties are cash cows, where the opportunity cost of having a film being shot might result in monetary losses that might take a long time to recover. Would the benefits ultimately outweigh the cost of not being operational for some time?

Turns out that letting films shoot on your property could reap huge rewards for the brand in the long run. To better understand how, one has to look at the hospitality industry at a micro level— look at individual hotels rather than looking at multiple properties.

We have to consider every hotel as an individual revenue centre, and like any other business, they have to ensure that they remain profitable at the end of the day. The general manager of the hotel and his team of departmental heads are responsible for ensuring that all his departments, the rooms, F&B, guest services, and sales and marketing are generating revenue on an ongoing basis.

To do so, they implement a variety of strategies that will attract guests to their property. These are generally a mix of online and offline activities that would lead to the generation of new business and guest loyalty programs that bring in regular footfall and room reservations through events such as weddings, conferences/ conventions, and other workshops. The internet has made it easier for them to showcase their properties to potential travellers anywhere in the world.

But that bell rings both ways. Competing properties have the same opportunities as you do. And you have to come up with more creative approaches to stay ahead in the game. You need a unique selling proposition that will make the property stand apart from the others and help you charge a higher tariff per night, one that your guest would happily pay.

Worldwide, movies have a reach like no other medium. They create an impact that could leave a mark on multiple generations. A single scene shot at your location could make your property legendary. Like I mentioned earlier, the gardens of the Taj Lake

Palace, Udaipur, that were featured in *Octopussy* become a huge hit with travellers from around the world, making it one of the most sought-after destination properties in India even today.

Similarly, when, in the movie *Pulp Fiction*, John Travolta tells Samual L. Jackson that you can buy a beer at a McDonald's in Paris, I remember that almost everyone wanted to go to Paris and order a beer at a McDonald's. That one scene had such a huge impact that it drove up the sales of beer at various McDonald's in Paris!

As a kid, my dad told me about this one time that an Indian film actor from the Kapoor's had come to their hotel for lunch. And from that day onwards, we always wanted to go to his hotel for lunches or dinners, hoping to see a celebrity in real life.

There's no denying that film-induced tourism is real, and letting films shoot on your property creates a ripple effect of positive word of mouth that can last several years. It pulls people in, gives you bragging rights, and certainly puts you a cut above the rest.

Now imagine Hrithik Roshan kicking John Abraham out of your hotel's fifth-floor room window in their next movie. Do you think this might push up your ratings? I bet it would.

Like they would say in the MasterCard Commercials:

The price of shutting your hotel for a day: ₹20 lakhs

The price of a broken window: ₹6000

The price of seeing John Abraham being kicked by Hrithik Roshan from your hotel window: PRICELESS!

Quality is never an accident. It is always
the result of an intelligent effort.

– John Ruskin

Contrasting Management Styles: Independent Hotels vs. Corporate Brand Hotels

By Anjalika Gupta

Independently-owned hotels provide a personal touch, flexibility, and a unique local identity while corporate brand hotels emphasise standardisation, established reputation, and ample resources. Guests can choose between an authentic, intimate experience or a consistent, globally recognised service based on their preferences and the hotel's management approach.

The hospitality industry encompasses a diverse range of establishments, from independently-owned boutique hotels to large hotel chains operated under corporate brand names. These two categories of hotels often exhibit distinctive management styles, each with its advantages and challenges. Understanding these differences is crucial for both hoteliers and guests to make informed decisions and have an enjoyable experience. Here, we will explore the contrasting management approaches of independently-owned hotels and corporate brand hotels.

Independently Owned Hotels

As the name suggests, independently-owned hotels are individual properties owned and operated by a single entity or a small group of investors. This category includes boutique hotels, bed-and-breakfasts, family-owned inns, or even large city hotels. Some of the renowned old forts and palaces are also owned and operated as independent hotels by the erstwhile rulers themselves.

The key features of the management style in independently owned hotels include the following:

- **Personal touch**: One of the most significant advantages of independently-owned hotels is the personal touch they provide. Owners are usually actively involved in day-to-day operations, and their passion and commitment often shine through in the services they offer. This hands-on approach fosters a warm and welcoming atmosphere, creating a unique and memorable experience for guests.

- **Flexibility and adaptability**: Independently-owned hotels have more freedom to make quick decisions and adapt to changing market or guest demands. They can respond rapidly to guest feedback, adjust pricing, and implement changes in amenities or services without navigating layers of bureaucracy, enabling a more agile and responsive management style.

- **Local character and identity**: These hotels tend to embody the local culture, history, and architecture of their surroundings, providing an authentic experience for guests. The focus on the locality creates a strong sense of place, making the hotel a reflection of its community and a destination in itself. This feature makes the hotels unique in their physical and cultural orientation. The cuisine and style of food presentation and service are rooted in the soil of the region, adding a flavour of authenticity.

- **Limited resources**: One of the challenges faced by independently-owned hotels is their limited resources compared to corporate brands. This can affect their ability to invest in extensive marketing campaigns, modern technology, or comprehensive staff training programs. This also limits their ability to grow into a multi-hotel company.

I would add here that the independent brand hotels owned by a large business group as part of their diversification program have no financial crunch or dearth of resources. Often, they divide the hotel business into two verticals: operations and back-of-the-house functions. While operations are left to the hoteliers, back-of-the-house functions have access to corporate resources. This provides them with a lovely synergy of expertise in management processes, systems, culture development, and planning.

Corporate Brand Hotels

Corporate brand hotels are part of a larger chain or franchise, or they are managed by a central corporate entity with an established brand. The key features of the management style in corporate brand hotels include the following:

- **Standardisation**: Corporate brand hotels pride themselves on consistency and standardised service across all their properties. Guests can expect a similar experience regardless of the location they choose. While standardisation of product specifications allows guests to know what to expect, which can be comforting for some travellers, these hotels also add the local dimension to the experience by way of furnishings, ambience, and availability of select local cuisine.

- **Established brand reputation**: Corporate brand hotels benefit from established brand reputations, often recognised globally. The power of the brand name attracts customers and helps build trust among guests, giving them confidence in their choice of accommodation. These hotels also run brand loyalty programs, which give them a loyal customer base.

- **Access to resources**: Corporate brands have access to substantial resources, including marketing budgets, state-of-the-art technology, and comprehensive human resource development programs. This enables them to reach a broader audience, implement the latest industry trends, and maintain high service standards

- **Best human resources**: Corporate brand hotels attract great talent who are exposed to standard, established management systems, development opportunities, and upward mobility. For brands with international presence, they also get the opportunity for horizontal mobility internationally.

- **Bureaucracy and rigidity**: The hierarchical structure of corporate brands can lead to bureaucracy and a slower decision-making process. This can hinder quick responses to local demands and challenges, making adaptation to specific markets more challenging.

In conclusion, the management styles of independently-owned hotels and corporate-brand hotels diverge significantly. While the former thrives on personal touch, adaptability, and local character, corporate brand hotels emphasize standardisation, established reputation, and access to extensive resources.

Both approaches have their strengths and weaknesses, catering to different preferences and needs of guests. Where, on the one hand, independently-owned hotels offer a more intimate and authentic experience, corporate brand hotels, on the other hand, provide a consistent and globally recognised service. Ultimately, the choice between the two styles depends on the individual preferences of guests and the specific goals of hotel owners and operators.

The Rise of Sleepcations: Rejuvenating Vacations for the Weary Traveller

By Pooja Ramanujan

The hospitality industry is witnessing the rise of a new group of travellers who're taking holidays for the specific reason of sleeping in. Known as 'sleepcations', this is a form of travel where hotel guests prioritise their sleep health over the desire to explore or go sightseeing.

Traditionally, vacations have been associated with sightseeing and adventure. Travellers would arrive at a location and then set off with a specific itinerary to explore the city, take in the culture, and carry back souvenirs. In recent years, however, a growing number of individuals have recognised the need for relaxation and rejuvenation as an essential part of their travel experiences. This has given rise to a new concept: sleepcation.

Combining the concepts of vacation and sleep, sleepcations offer travellers the chance to unwind, recharge, and prioritise their sleep in a serene and comfortable environment, where they can find solace, address their sleep-related concerns, and return home feeling refreshed and revitalised.

In today's fast-paced and demanding world, finding time for rest and relaxation has become an essential part of maintaining overall well-being. With an increasing number of individuals recognising the importance of quality sleep, hotels around the world have responded by providing a host of amenities and services designed to enhance the sleep experience of their guests.

So what has brought about this change in preferences among travellers?

There are various factors that have compromised the quality of sleep, the biggest one being the Covid-19 pandemic that brought the world to a halt in 2020. The resultant quarantine, isolation, social distancing, and changing lifestyles led to an increase in anxiety levels, which in turn impacted people's quality of sleep.

The next biggest cause is the general pressures associated with modern lifestyles. Excessive screen time, longer work hours, and increased work pressure have led to irregular sleep patterns and taken a toll on mental well-being. As a result, people are experiencing a greater need to address their sleep issues, looking for new ways to alleviate stress by finding solace in tranquil environments. Sleepcations offer a purposeful break from the disturbances and distractions of daily life, allowing travellers to prioritise self-care and enjoy more restful nights.

How are hotels catering to the rising demand for sleepcations?

To cater to the rising demand for sleep-oriented vacations, hotels have taken significant strides in creating environments conducive to a good night's sleep. Recognising that comfort is of paramount importance, these establishments have invested in a range of amenities and services designed to enhance the sleep experience.

- **Choice of pillows:** One size does not fit all when it comes to pillows. Hotels now understand the importance of offering a variety of pillow options to cater to individual preferences. Guests can select from an extensive menu of pillows, including memory foam, hypoallergenic, and feather pillows, ensuring a personalised and comfortable sleep experience.

- **High-quality bed linen:** Hotels have come to realise that the quality of bed linen can significantly impact the quality of sleep. To provide guests with a superior sleeping environment, many establishments now offer premium thread count sheets, soft duvets, and plush mattress toppers. These high-quality linens create a luxurious and cosy atmosphere, promoting restful sleep.

- **Blackout curtains and soundproofing:** Recognising the importance of minimising external disturbances, hotels are implementing blackout curtains and soundproofing techniques to create a serene sleeping environment. These features ensure that guests can enjoy uninterrupted sleep, shielded from unwanted light and noise that may disrupt their rest.

- **Sleep-enhancing amenities:** Some hotels go the extra mile by providing sleep-enhancing amenities, such as aromatherapy kits, white noise machines, and relaxation apps. These thoughtful additions help guests relax and create a peaceful ambience, facilitating a deeper and more rejuvenating sleep.

- **Sleep-friendly technology:** Technology has also played a role in enhancing the sleep experience. Many hotels now offer adjustable mattresses, smart lighting systems, and temperature control options in guest rooms. These technological advancements allow guests to customise their sleeping environment according to their preferences, ensuring maximum comfort and restfulness.

- **Sleep-focused programs:** Hotels are increasingly focusing on holistic wellness by incorporating sleep-focused programs, which include partnering with sleep experts and wellness practitioners to provide tailored sleep assessments, relaxation techniques, and sleep-inducing spa treatments.

By offering personalised sleep solutions, hotels aim to create a memorable and rejuvenating experience that goes beyond a typical vacation.

In an increasingly fast-paced world, the need for quality sleep has gained recognition as a fundamental aspect of overall well-being. The sleepcation trend has emerged as a response to this growing awareness, providing individuals with an opportunity to focus on rest and rejuvenation during their vacations. As it continues to gain momentum, individuals seeking respite from their hectic lives can look forward to an array of options that prioritise their sleep and well-being.

Keen to cater to this evolving trend, the hospitality industry is proactively preparing for the future of sleepcations. They are continuously innovating and expanding their offerings to provide guests with an exceptional sleep experience. Forward-thinking hotels are investing in cutting-edge sleep technologies and advanced amenities to create sleep-friendly environments that meet the evolving needs of travellers. In addition to technological advancements and wellness initiatives, hotels are also likely to continue refining their sleep-related amenities and services. They will place greater emphasis on providing customised sleep experiences through an expanded range of pillow options, luxurious bed linens, and soothing sleep-enhancing products.

The future of sleepcations looks promising. This is not a passing trend that we are looking at. In fact, this is a reflection of our evolving understanding of the crucial role sleep plays in our overall health and happiness. With increasing importance being placed on sleep and well-being, coupled with hotels' proactive response to this trend, sleepcations are poised to grow and evolve. As hotels continue to innovate and refine their offerings to provide exceptional sleep experiences, travellers can expect even more immersive and rejuvenating sleepcation options in the years to come.

ISBN Number: 978-1-64733-913-5